HAPPINESS BY NUMBERS

Happiness
By
Numbers

How to measure and manage your wellbeing
to make a positive impact on the world

To Dawn + Jim,

best wishes from

Richard

R A Lupo

Richard Lupo

Happiness by Numbers
ISBN 978-1-915483-08-9
eISBN 978-1-915483-09-6

Published in 2023 by Right Book Press
Printed in the UK

A CIP record of this book is available from the British Library.

Contents

I'd like to dedicate this book to the most important people in my life. My wonderful and patient daughter Megan, who now knows more about Maslow than she ever wanted. My lovely mum Marlene, who will no doubt tell all her friends that 'her son' has written a published book. And my beautiful partner Rachael who has brought whole new dimensions of happiness into our conversations. These lovely ladies are helping me edge towards 10 out of 10 for my own happiness.

By the end of this book you will be able to answer these questions about your own long-term wellbeing (see also page 9):

Question	Your answer
Marks out of 50, how far are your basic needs met?	
Marks out of 25, how far are your security needs met?	
Marks out of 10, how satisfied are you with your social life?	
Marks out of 10, how worthwhile are the things you do?	
Marks out of 5, how satisfied are you with your amount of leisure time?	
Your long-term wellbeing (%)	

As you work through the book, return here to keep a record of your answers. Add up the numbers to arrive at the total to enter at the bottom.

Introduction

One thing is certain: we all want to be happy. Ideally, we also want our friends and loved ones to be happy. And for the most altruistic of us, we'd love for everyone in the world to be happy. In fact, we'd like 100 per cent of us to be 100 per cent happy for 100 per cent of our lifetimes. But how do we define '100 per cent happiness'? Maybe you think we can't – after all, happiness is subjective, isn't it? Calculating it as a percentage is impossible. But, as the title of this book suggests, there is in fact a way to define happiness in numbers. And the numbers part is important because, as we shall see, being able to *measure* happiness means we can *manage* our happiness.

The great thing is that we humans are biologically programmed to pursue our own happiness. We seek pleasure in the form of food, entertainment, security and relationships. It's the purpose of each and every one of us. Part of our evolution has come from balancing our own happiness with that of those around us – including our own planet. Can we be 100 per cent happy if we are destroying the people and environment around us? How much emphasis should we place on our own comfort and how much on that of others? Where does our pleasure-seeking behaviour start negatively affecting our own happiness? When it comes to balancing our own happiness with the wellbeing of the planet, how do we know when we've got it right?

We all know we ought to do something to help the planet and we all probably do our own little bit. We may also think that we could do more. But how much is enough? Contrary to what you might think, this 'sweet spot' *is* something we can measure. And what we can measure, we can control. This book is a blueprint to achieve both a happy life and an environmentally sound one. It asks the question, how do we work out how to maximise our own comfort and convenience while still caring for the wellbeing of the planet?

I will explore how it's possible to measure various aspects of life followed by chapters offering practical measures to improve these aspects. The book also offers ways to measure your own progress towards happiness, a tool to see where you are now and to measure how far your actions will take you.

The book falls into two halves. Chapters 1–4 are about understanding how we can measure happiness in different areas of our lives. Chapters 5–9 are made up of practical suggestions for how to raise our levels of long-term wellbeing.

I will look at the data in order to concentrate on the gaps revealed by that data and suggest changes accordingly. This will go some way to help readers with things that they may be struggling with, such as:

- making a house fit for the future
- doing what makes you happy but in a more sustainable way
- having money yet not feeling happy
- a feeling like there should be more, that something is missing.

Most of what you will find here is applicable at an individual and/or household level. But you might also be in a position of authority within an organisation, in which case there's a section on how you can help other people achieve the same (see Chapter 9). Imagine if we could cascade this thinking to everyone – from household to household, business to business, council to council, authority to authority. We would not only all be a lot better off but so would future generations of our loved ones and friends.

The truth is that we cannot separate our own happiness from the wellbeing of the planet. For the purposes of this book, 'the environment' is the planet, the natural world and the ecosystems that act within it. We know about some of the ecological issues facing us and why they're so important for 'the environment'. But most important are the knock-on effects. After all, the environment doesn't really care what we do to it – it will continue to exist in one form or another. But if we damage it too much, will it be a suitable environment for humans to live in? *Homo sapiens* is a newcomer to our planet – we have only been here for a few hundred thousand years. In the four billion years before that, the planet carried on quite happily, with lots of different environments suitable for lots of other living species – from tiny microbes to meat-eating dinosaurs. It didn't matter to anyone that *Homo sapiens* wasn't one of them.

But it now matters to us. In fact, our happiness depends on it.

So how do we as a species make ourselves happier? The answer is in measurement.

Manage what you measure

I used to work in manufacturing plants with intricate quality assurance systems. These systems were important because they ensured the quality of the final products. After all, some of these products were to end up in aeroplane engines, nuclear power plants, pharmaceutical devices, domestic drinking water systems and Ministry of Defence equipment. Making sure they were high quality was a big deal.

Key to these quality systems was measurement. We measured everything – from the diameter of tubes to the cleanliness of air inside pharmaceutical clean rooms. Some of our instruments were pretty low tech, such as micrometers. But other equipment was intricate and could involve ultrasonic inspection probes or complex chemical analyses. The measurements provided assurance that our production systems were correct and that is what justified the resource and investment in both the quality assurance systems and the measurement devices used within them. Measurement also showed where things were going wrong so timely corrections could be made.

The key mantra was 'you can only manage what you measure'. So if there was a change to a manufacturing process, we measured the outcomes. If there was a research trial, we measured the outcomes. Only if the outcomes were positive could we introduce the findings into the mainstream manufacturing.

If we, a world of eight billion humans, want to be happy, the most effective method would be to take some of the learning from manufacturing and apply it to our long-term aim of 100 per cent happiness. Once we start measuring happiness in a consistent manner – and that measure includes environmental protection – then we can start to see what works to improve it and what doesn't have any impact. This is crucial because there can be a big difference between what we *think* will work and what *actually* works.

A seafaring tale

In the 1700s, the British Navy worked out that it was losing more sailors to scurvy than in battle. Top physicians at the time recommended cures such as bloodletting and even eating faeces. But still thousands of sailors were dying. A young naval surgeon at the time, James Lind, decided to take a different tack. He organised a trial where sailors who had scurvy symptoms were allocated different treatments. He tested six cures, one of which was eating citrus fruit. This was added to the trial as an afterthought as it was considered to have little chance of success. The symptoms of each group of patients were monitored and compared at the end of the trial. It was only then that the surgeon found that the sailors who ate the fruit quickly regained their health compared to their unfortunate shipmates in the other trial groups.

The science of wellbeing?

But is wellbeing truly something we can measure? The short answer is yes. In this book you'll learn about some of the latest developments in the science of wellbeing and its measurement. Because there really is a science behind it. And the good thing about a science base is that it is more likely to reflect the truth than any particular individual's assertions.

However, there is a downside. The emerging science of wellbeing predominantly focuses on individuals' *feelings* of happiness – in other words, subjective wellbeing. This means it leaves out physical realities such as the likelihood of being physically attacked or, more relevant for this book, the likelihood of our environment no longer being able to support humans.

Thankfully there is an even older scientific framework that includes both the physical aspects of our long-term wellbeing plus how we actually feel. What's more, this familiar framework lends itself to measurement. It's called Maslow's hierarchy and it will be fully explored in Chapter 1. It also supplies the structure for the measurements explored in the book.

The silt road

My discovery of the wellbeing agenda came about when I was carrying out research at Imperial College London. My project was to find a use for thousands of tonnes of waste silt generated by the aggregate processing industry. A lot of the aggregate was either extracted from excavation soil from construction projects, crushing of waste concrete or, in some cases, digging up previously landfilled construction waste. In order for the aggregate to be useful it had to be washed to remove very fine particles of clay and silt which would otherwise affect the aggregate's physical properties. The wash water was filtered and the resulting silt was dumped because there was no other use for it.

I started to develop a process that mixed the waste silt with cement. This would strengthen it enough so that it too could be used for aggregate instead of simply ending up in landfill. As part of the project I completed a sustainability assessment. This included looking at the embodied energy of the materials used in the process, together with other environmental issues such as water use to see if this was an environmentally sound solution.

The assessment revealed that the cement had a high CO_2 content. This gave us a dilemma: should we divert thousands of tonnes of waste from landfill (good) but have to use CO_2-intensive cement to do so (bad)? Or would it be better to just let it go to landfill (bad) so we don't incur the CO_2 penalty of cement (good)?

At the time similar analyses were being carried out to decide whether or not to clear up sites of contaminated land. A suggested approach was to convert the pros and cons of the different options into a pounds and pence figure. For example, the main con of clearing up a contaminated site was the cost, whereas one of the main pros was the profit from being able to develop the site. To bump up the pros, project managers tried to establish 'willingness to pay' figures for local people in the area who would pay extra to have access to the new land without their children getting harmed. Then they added on the increase in house prices around the contaminated site.

It seems a logical approach but on deeper analysis, it is fraught with difficulties. For example, is the cost–benefit analysis the best way to evaluate whether or not a dangerous site should be remediated? How attainable is the money calculated? The developer might pay for the remediation but it's the local homeowners who will benefit. And who gains from the 'willingness to pay' benefits? No money is actually changing hands. I started to think about basing decisions on happiness or wellbeing. Could this be measured?

The social value problem

We've certainly tried. The UK Public Services (Social Values) Act 2012 requires people who commission public services to think about how they can also secure wider social, economic and environmental benefits. This has spurred a whole industry that attempts to capture social value. Although not required to, many of the companies who tender for public contracts employ techniques to evaluate their contribution to social value – again, in pounds and pence. The calculations go along the lines of:

1. We do a schoolroom talk to educate children about how to get a job.
2. This makes an x per cent contribution to 30 children getting a job, which adds £y to the UK economy.
3. Therefore the social value we bring is £z of our staff time at the school + the £ value to the economy.

This calculation is repeated for a variety of 'social value' activities that the company may do until they have a final figure of, say, £100,000 of social value. This goes on their tender and the public body evaluating tenders takes this 'social value' into account. But nobody gets the extra £100,000. Is this really improving things? And even if it is, is £100,000 enough? Is it too much?

There is a similar approach called social return on investment (SROI). It goes through similar calculations to figure out how much money a particular activity is worth. But again, it generates a pounds and pence value that no one can get their hands on. Furthermore, there's no mechanism to check whether social value has actually increased after the project is carried out.

And then there is the problem of inflation. Another scheme uses similar calculations to SROI but this time it models the wellbeing increases to the recipients of a particular activity. These wellbeing increases are then given a degree of attribution to the project and summed to give an overall wellbeing increase score for however many people may benefit from that project. This figure is converted into pounds and pence based on a scale of how much money an increase in wellbeing is worth. So we are back to pounds and pence. You could end up with a value of £200,000 this year but this won't be an absolute figure because inflation will change its value over years. In other words, a project (eg a new community centre) may increase the wellbeing of 100 people by one point. This figure will be the same regardless of the year it gets built. By applying pounds and pence, we have to accept that this value will change over time, unlike, say, an absolute measure like centimetres and metres. So reducing benefits to pounds and pence makes them meaningless over time.

A matrix for happiness

To summarise, there isn't currently an established method of measuring wellbeing that incorporates environmental sustainability. The measures that do exist either use money as a surrogate for wellbeing or do not include environmental impacts. What's needed is a measure that combines all these issues, is science based and has a chance of becoming widely accepted. Who knows, such a measure could eventually replace money as the be-all-and-end-all measure of what life is all about.

I don't pretend to have developed such a system, but I will share with you a measure that will give you some idea of the impact our actions and behaviours can have on our environment and our happiness.

Throughout the book I am going to use a matrix like the one below for you to record your answers. I've put the average answers for the UK in there already, as well as what the ideal answer would be. As soon as you start filling in the matrix you'll have a so-called gap analysis – you will see the gap between the ideal and what you do now. As you go through the book, you'll find tips on how to fill those gaps. So, by the end of the book you'll have a blueprint for, if not living happily ever after, then getting pretty close to it.

Question	Average UK answer	Ideal answer	Your answer
Marks out of 50 how far are your basic needs met?	50.0	50	??
Marks out of 25, how far are your security needs met?	20.7	25	??
Marks out of 10, how satisfied are you with your social life?	7.0	10	??
Marks out of 10, how worthwhile are the things you do?	7.8	10	??
Marks out of 5, how satisfied are you with your amount of leisure time?	0.7	5	??
Total	86.2	100	

You'll see in later chapters how I arrived at the UK average values and how you can fill out your own answers in the table on page vii. When you discover your gap analysis you will be a lot closer to understanding how to meet the combined aims of a happy, sustainable life. You'll be surprised to know that in most cases it is not one thing at the expense of another.

At first glance, you might be thinking that 86.2 out of 100 for our long-term wellbeing looks pretty good. And you'd be right – we have a lot to be grateful for in this country: our lights come on when we flip the switch, water comes out of our taps, we are not in a war zone. But on the other hand, if we are achieving less than 100 out of 100, we will suffer in the long term. We might even descend into not satisfying our basic needs.

This book contains lots of numbers, targets and lists. That's deliberate because, as I stated earlier, what we can measure we can manage. There are lots of examples where it is difficult to decide between different options. For example:

- Should we use paper towels in public bathrooms and generate waste or should we use electric driers and cause CO_2 emissions?
- Is it better to knock down older, inefficient buildings and build new energy efficient ones? What about the embodied energy in the materials? What about the aesthetic considerations?
- Should we use reusable nappies that have to be washed regularly or carry on with easy-to-use disposable ones?
- Should we sacrifice our comfort by installing rainwater harvesting systems or composting toilets?

By the end of the book, you'll have a better way of deciding these things for yourself.

How much is enough? The interactions between humans and the planet and the environment create a hugely complex system. For example, while we are pursuing wealth which, according to old assumptions, makes us happier, we are slowly damaging our environment. Damaging our environment means that we pollute our air, water and soil to the extent that it starts to affect our health, which is bad for our long-term wellbeing.

On the other hand, having a framework to look at the whole delivers a neat way to categorise the issues and deal with them in order of importance. Happiness itself has a dual benefit: as well as the feeling of happiness itself, striving for happiness can also help protect our environment. For instance, buying fewer products is not only good for the environment (and therefore good for your long-term wellbeing) but it frees you from clutter, worry and decision making. So you can do without that electric photo frame.

Of course, this doesn't mean we must never buy anything ever again. There are many items we really need: food, homes to live in, ways to maintain a comfortable body temperature. But there are discretionary items we can choose between, and we'll be looking at that in later chapters.

A better way

Our happiness is inextricably linked to the wellbeing of our planet. To maximise both, we need to measure the impacts of our behaviour on our own lives and the environment around us and take steps to rebalance our footprint on the world. When we do, we will find that our measurements of wellbeing increase, not just in the short term but for the centuries ahead.

So let's look at some numbers.

One last note

Unless stated otherwise, most of the data is UK based. No doubt there will be equivalent datasets for other countries but the principles of this blueprint work for everyone on the planet.

Throughout the book I use happiness, wellbeing and social value interchangeably. In the 'What's in a name?' section in Chapter 1 (see p15) we'll look at the nuances but most of the time they are interchangeable terms.

Chapter 1
Can we measure happiness?

In this chapter I will look at definitions of happiness and the different ways that people have attempted to measure it over time. I will try to assess how environmental factors impact happiness and then propose a new measure based on scoring how far the basic needs of humans are being met.

Our quest to measure happiness is relatively new. In fact, the story starts shortly after the Second World War, when international powers sought to reconstruct a broken world. As a means to continually check the success (or otherwise) of individual government policies, they devised a measure called gross domestic product (GDP). GDP is a monetary measure of the value of all final goods and services produced in a period of time (quarterly or yearly). As an aid to reconstructing homes and providing food for the broken countries after the war, this proved a reasonable enough approach. However, using GDP as a measure of wellbeing came into question once those basic needs of society had been fulfilled.

Even the Bank of England recognises that GDP is imperfect (2019). For instance, GDP increases if there is a war, because a nation will spend huge amounts on ammunition and other military hardware and personnel. But that doesn't translate into an increase in wellbeing. And what about nations that make huge sums from sales of timber from environmentally sensitive rainforests? Again, that doesn't mean its residents are happier.

Some of the most rigorous questioning of the GDP approach came from economist Professor Richard Easterlin. In his work (1974) he found that economic indicators (of which GDP is one) did not correlate with the happiness or welfare of people. This was based on scientific data and led to what is now called the Easterlin Paradox. He recognised that many factors contribute to happiness and income is only one of them. Since then a whole branch of happiness economics and psychology has evolved and different measurements of elements of wellbeing have been established (see Tay & Diener 2011, for example).

The group Action for Happiness (actionforhappiness.org), co-founded by Lord Richard Layard, professor of economics at the London School of Economics and author of *Happiness: Lessons from a new science* (2005), has previously noted that there are correlations between people's self-reported happiness and blood pressure, heart rates, immune system responses, brain activity and independent assessments given by friends and family, all suggesting that our subjective experiences have objective reality.

This suggests that wellbeing is not only a measurable concept but its measurement is taken seriously at international levels. In time, happiness measurements have the potential to replace GDP as a fuller measure of success of governments' policies.

However, currently in the UK, statistics on wellbeing are simply a collection of figures gleaned from surveys. They cover a variety of issues such as physical health, unemployment and crime statistics and there are even figures on waste recycling and carbon emissions reported in the same datasets. What's missing is a single figure of wellbeing synthesised from all the individual measures. The framework presented in this book is a proposal to develop a single synthesised figure. For this to work, the data will be down to individual or household level. However, the methodology could be scaled to any population size.

Happiness is a real, measurable concept and, in this context, it should be taken to mean wellbeing in its widest sense. That includes physical wellbeing, such as sufficient food supply and adequate thermal comfort, but also emotional wellbeing, which includes social contact as well as other aspects of mental wellness.

What's in a name?

Up to this point I've been using the words happiness, wellbeing and social value interchangeably. I guess we all have a good sense of our own definition of happiness. Nevertheless it is worth looking at different definitions.

Happiness

Some positive psychologists split happiness into two categories, namely hedonic happiness and eudaimonic happiness. Hedonic happiness is about pleasure and enjoyment but eudaimonic happiness is about having meaning and purpose in our lives. In any case, they believe that we all need a bit of both.

Wellbeing

The Organisation for Economic Co-operation and Development (OECD) is a respected body, with most countries in the world being members. Its goal is 'to shape policies that foster prosperity, equality, opportunity and wellbeing for all'. Encouragingly, even though it focuses on economics, it has also done a large amount of work on wellbeing, including collecting statistics on the subject. It hasn't defined wellbeing yet but one of its early papers acknowledges:

All people have aspirations for themselves and for their children to live better lives. While it is important that people have enough food and their basic needs are met it is also important that the roundedness of their efforts to live well and with dignity is not overlooked in international development policy. (OECD 2013)

Social value

When we talk about social value we often think of aspects of life that cannot be bought: access to fresh air, a safe and clean environment, equal opportunities and access to healthcare. But social value has not been defined by the UK government. The nearest thing we have to legislation for wellbeing in England is the Public Services (Social Value) Act which, as we saw in the Introduction, requires 'people who commission public services to think about how they can also secure wider social, economic and environmental benefits'. Here is a list of themes (from GCF 2020) which will give an idea of the Act's intentions:

- Covid-19 recovery
- tackling economic inequality
- fighting climate change
- equal opportunity
- wellbeing (improving health and wellbeing but more about avoiding sickness).

In Wales, the Wellbeing of Future Generations Act also has no soundbite definition and local areas are left to define wellbeing around seven core goals (Welsh Government 2022):

1. a prosperous Wales
2. a resilient Wales
3. a more equal Wales
4. a healthier Wales

5. a Wales of cohesive communities

6. a Wales of vibrant culture and thriving Welsh language

7. a globally responsible Wales.

Other countries have also recognised the importance of wellbeing without accurately defining it. In Bhutan, the king famously declared that 'Gross National Happiness is more important than Gross Domestic Product'. Since then the country has developed a Gross National Happiness Index which combines a series of 33 indicators covering nine domains (similar to the lists for Wales and England above) – see gnhcentrebhutan.org/gnh-happiness-index/. In addition there are a few non-government schemes globally: One Planet Living, the Happy Planet Index and the Happy City Index to name a few.

So, although many organisations and countries are taking the matter seriously, as yet no single definition of wellbeing has emerged. However, we all have a pretty good idea of what it means. Not all schemes mentioned above combine separate metrics into a single wellbeing figure and some do recognise the importance of environmental protection. And most are based at a national level which makes it pretty hard to measure happiness individually.

Although definitions of wellbeing vary, for the purposes of this book, I use American psychologist Abraham Maslow's hierarchy of needs (see the 'Maslow to the rescue' section below). If an individual has all those needs 100 per cent satisfied, then that is 100 per cent wellbeing achieved. All other definitions and frameworks I've seen can be easily mapped onto this framework.

Happiness of nations

On a national level, the OECD has been doing interesting work. It agreed in 2007 to form a shared view of societal wellbeing by collecting and reporting statistics on societal progress. This has manifested itself in many countries and now the UK Government's

Office of National Statistics (ONS) releases wellbeing statistics each year. This supports the assertion that 'measuring' wellbeing is a real, tangible thing that we can (and should) do.

For example, the ONS conducts life satisfaction surveys which ask people to rate their lives on a scale from 0 (not at all satisfied) to 10 (completely satisfied). This question is repeated for many OECD countries, which allows international comparison.

I'll look at how happy we are now in later chapters but just as a taster, here are the answers to this particular question given in the latest OECD 'How's life?' report (OECD 2020), in which 34 countries were asked:

- Average: 7.4
- UK: 7.6
- Worst: Turkey 5.7
- Best: Columbia 8.3

There are the usual caveats about methodological differences and some exclusions due to lack of data – for example, Chile, Israel, Japan and the United States did not supply data for this survey. But it shows that the idea of measuring wellbeing is gaining ground and a metric has even appeared in the UK Government's Treasury Green Book. The Green Book allows policymakers to evaluate impacts of suggested policies on things that have not been taken into account. It still relies on conversion into pounds and pence but at least there are beginning to be standard conversions and if the typically non-financial benefits (eg wellbeing) are converted to money and that value is more than the cost of the policy, this will support the policy's implementation.

Interesting snippets from the Green Book include:

People are all different and age, gender and genetics all affect wellbeing. Evidence suggests that between a third and a half of the variation in wellbeing within a population is fixed, presumed to stem from people's genetic makeup. The remainder can be partially explained by other factors. (HM Treasury 2021)

The Green Book also has values for carbon emissions, with a tonne of carbon being assigned a value of £245. So, if a policy has the potential to result in fewer carbon emissions, it is seen as saving £245 per tonne. (Incidentally, that is the central estimate for 2021; the high-end estimate for 2050 is £568 per tonne.)

Don't forget the environment!

But although measuring wellbeing in one form or another does seem to be being carried out at various levels, aside from the possible inclusion of the Bhutanese Gross National Happiness Index, these measures of wellbeing don't include a measure of environmental protection. Yet this is vital when measuring our medium- and long-term wellbeing.

In *Collapse: How societies choose to Fail or Succeed* (2005), Jared Diamond catalogues historical civilisations that have collapsed, mainly because they either didn't adapt to the environmental conditions they were in or did not protect it. For example, Mayan and Easter Island cultures believed in and relied on praying to gods for good crops. They did this instead of preserving water supplies and protecting the forests on their land. In fact, some of the last trees on Easter Island were felled in order to roll the famous Easter Island statues to the sites deemed best to please the gods.

In Greenland, a Viking community was wiped out because it insisted on eating beef. The Vikings never got a taste for the seal meat that was a staple diet for local native people but they did not take into account that Greenland's climate is not suited to cattle rearing because it can't grow sufficient hay to provide food for cattle while they are kept in barns over the winter.

In more recent times, evidence of the beginnings of the collapse of societies has been very real. In the early 2010s a series of revolutions, protests and armed rebellions swept the Arab world and became collectively known as the Arab Spring. The uprisings had many contributing factors but one was crop failures and the consequent increase in food prices (Perez 2013). The region imports food from places such as Russia and Canada but a combination of storms and droughts in those countries – caused largely by climate change – led to decreased supplies of food.

In other words, we have to protect and live within our environmental means if we hope to reap the benefits of living in these societies for our future and for future generations.

Invent a unit of measurement

Subjective wellbeing units of measurement are emerging for how individuals feel about themselves. The WELLBY is a unit of measurement that combines current wellbeing on a scale from 0 to 10 then pairs it with life expectancy (Layard & Oparina 2021). In so doing, it measures a 'wellbeing year', accounting for both the quality and longevity of human life.

There are also numerous environmental measures but there isn't a single universally accepted measure of wellbeing. And there is even less in the way of measures that can be applied down to household level. Wouldn't it be useful to have a new metric that we could all use and count up on a regular basis? We could use it to track how we are doing and make improvements for ourselves, while at the same time improving the world for our children and loved ones.

Maslow to the rescue

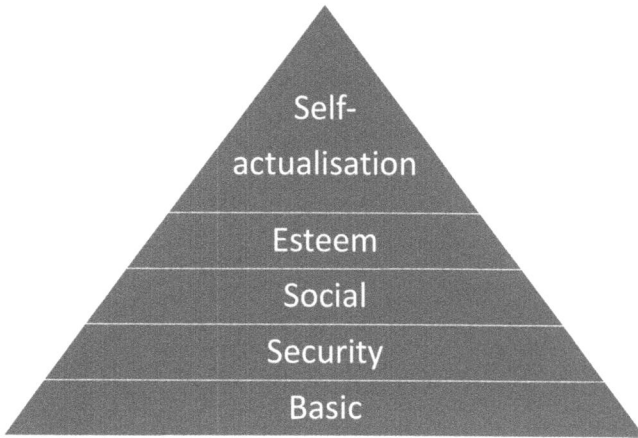

Maslow's hierarchy of needs is a well-known and accepted description of human needs.

Maslow was an American clinical and research psychologist in the 1940s and 50s whose clinical work involved treating people with psychological illnesses. From this work he derived his now famous hierarchy of human needs (Maslow 1943).

He found that once people had satisfied a need on the lower level of the hierarchy – say, food – they would aim to satisfy the needs on the next level. Once they reached the top level of the pyramid, the ultimate need was for something Maslow termed 'self-actualisation'. Maslow's hierarchy is particularly useful because the needs are independent of culture and values – they are simply based on what humans strive for.

Briefly, here are Maslow's needs:

- ▲ Basic – as the name suggests, these are our fundamental needs. Without them, humans would die pretty quickly. They comprise necessities such as food, water, air and thermal comfort. Maslow also classed reproduction as a basic need.

- ▲ Security – for the purposes of using Maslow as a framework, this is interpreted as meaning the security of supply of our basic needs as well as security against physical attack.
- ▲ Social – Maslow found that humans need to be in contact with other humans or their mental wellbeing suffers.
- ▲ Esteem – this means respect from our peers. Without societal respect, our mental health also suffers.
- ▲ Self-actualisation. This is a state where we constantly enjoy many peak experiences. This need can be satisfied in different ways for different people and indeed Maslow gives a range of examples. People who have attained self-actualisation might include senior professionals and politicians but also homemakers who have found the perfect arrangement of their furniture. This isn't intended to be a flippant comment. The point is that you don't need to have a high-flying job to experience self-actualisation.

Importantly, in general humans will not seek to satisfy a higher need until a lower need in the hierarchy is satisfied. Maslow also recognised that there would be fluctuations between hierarchical levels and some people may skip a few levels depending on their personal priorities. For example, an artist might go without food while painting their best picture. However, in general, Maslow holds true.

Maslow's theories are widely accepted and often used in motivational teaching for business managers. However, they are based on clinical and psychological fieldwork and recent research strongly supports Maslow's theory that these needs are universal for all humans on the planet (Tay & Diener 2011).

For the purposes of our proposed wellbeing measurement, existing data on a population can be categorised into each of Maslow's needs. This enables us to calculate the 'percentage of needs met'. This is the wellbeing measure. This can be applied to individuals, groups of people such as organisations and social groups, and even nations. The approach is detailed below:

1. Evaluate the extent to which Maslow's needs are satisfied in the group, starting at the lowest level and working to the top. If 100 per cent of those needs are met, then you have 100 per cent wellbeing. (All needs are considered, including food security, social needs and esteem.)
2. Combine all the metrics using weightings to reflect the importance of each layer.

Below I outline the process of quantification for each step. They are presented in the order of Maslow's needs: basic, security, social, esteem and self-actualisation.

I have described examples of how to measure the extent to which individual needs of humans are met. I have also described how our environmental impacts affect our ability to satisfy our own security needs in particular, which is further covered in Chapter 3. These measures then need to be combined into a single measure of gross wellbeing.

For basic and security needs, there are several sub-needs to be measured and met (food, water, air, thermal comfort and security from physical attack). It would be reasonable to average these, which has been done in the security section. Before averaging the distinct tiers, it is first necessary to weight them. This would give more weight to more basic needs as these are more important than, say, self-actualisation.

There is no academic data to indicate what these weightings should be for our overall wellbeing but from a small survey of my own I found that most people considered the following weightings to be appropriate:

- basic: 50 per cent
- security: 25 per cent
- social: 10 per cent
- esteem: 10 per cent
- self-actualisation: 5 per cent.

The figures in this table were based on the wellbeing survey data and environmental protection data available when I first developed the metric:

Need	Degree of need that is satisfied (%)	Weighting	Weighted degree (need satisfaction x weighting) (%)
Basic	100	0.50 (or 50%)	100 x 0.5 = **50.0**
Security	82.7	0.25 (or 25%)	82.7 x 0.25 = **20.7**
Social	70	0.10 (or 10%)	70 x 0.1 = **7.0**
Esteem	30.1	0.10 (or 10%)	30.1 x 0.1 = **3.0**
Self-actualisation	13.6	0.05 (or 5%)	13.6 x 0.05 = **0.7**
Overall wellbeing			Sum of the above = **81.4**

For those not mathematically minded another way to look at the table above is:

- basic – marks out of 50 was 50
- security – marks out of 25 was 20.7
- social – marks out of 10 was 7
- esteem – marks out of 10 was 3
- self-actualisation – marks out of 5 was 0.7.

In this example, using this proposed methodology, the person's overall wellbeing was 81.4 per cent. By the end of this book you'll be able to give yourself an overall score using this framework.

It is important to note that not all needs at one level need to be 100 per cent met before the next layer can be achieved. For example, we may forgo a small bit of security and still pursue social contact. This is useful, as the measure lends itself to assessing whole populations of people: the measure would highlight where most people don't have these needs met and hence highlight where any interventions would provide the most wellbeing.

In the earliest version of this metric I had the idea that we could calculate our own wellbeing then subtract the 'illbeing' our actions might cause others to create a figure of 'net wellbeing'. For example, what are the impacts of carbon emissions from the developed world on people in other countries (see Lupo 2020)? Let's look at how this might work.

The carbon effect

In developed countries, arguably the greatest impact on the environment is from carbon emissions from built environments. Excess emissions lead to uncontrolled climate change which leads to drought, floods, heatwaves and sea level rises (we have seen that these are already affecting the security of supply of our basic needs).

The good news is that making the world a happy place seems to be recognised at United Nations level as part of the plan to keep climate change at a safe level. The Intergovernmental Panel on Climate Change (IPCC) is the United Nation's body for assessing the science related to climate change. The IPCC's report made the headlines (IPCC 2021). It confirmed that climate change is real, it presents adverse effects to us all and it is caused by human activity. For environmental professionals this was hardly news but it was good to see the topic gaining even more media attention. The key question is what to do about it. The IPCC will continue to release reports on this. For now, I have looked at some of the detail in the current report that reveals some surprising possible ways forward.

To look into the future, the IPCC uses a range of different scenarios to analyse what might happen. Data from the scenarios is fed into various climate models and the outputs plotted to project what °C warming each scenario will lead to. The chart below is taken from the report and shows the impact of each of the scenarios. Each scenario (called a shared socioeconomic pathway or SSP) has a label SSP1-1.9 to SSP5-8.5.

(a) Global surface temperature change relative to 1850–1900

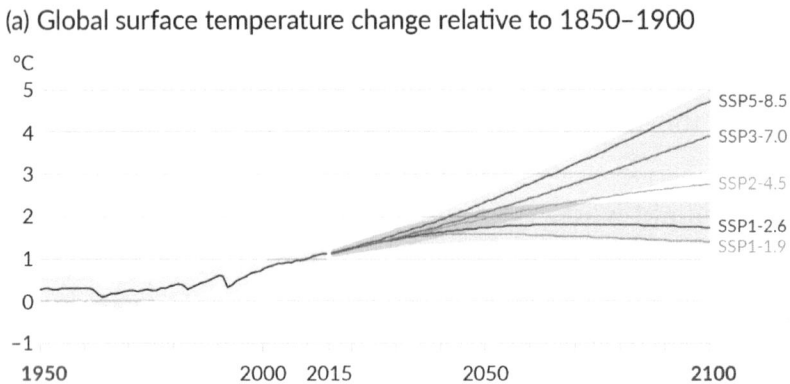

Only scenario SSP1-1.9 results in maintaining global temperatures to safe(ish) levels (ie less than 1.5°C rise in surface temperature). Here are the headlines of what SS1-1.9 means (Riahi et al. 2017):

- ⋏ gradual but pervasive shift toward a sustainable path
- ⋏ inclusive development that respects perceived environmental boundaries
- ⋏ management of global commons slowly improves
- ⋏ education and health investments accelerate the demographic transition, leading to a relatively low world

population (interaction of low mortality rates, improved education – especially women, fertility)

⅄ economic growth shifts toward a broader emphasis on human wellbeing

⅄ consumption is oriented toward low material growth and lower resource and energy intensity.

What's particularly interesting is the idea of transforming the world economic system for the benefit of human wellbeing instead of the current paradigm of maximising profit. Incidentally, one of the very first definitions of sustainable development incorporates both environmental protection and human needs. It is the so-called Brundtland definition, coined by former Norwegian premier Gro Brundtland as part of her world commission on environment and development in 1987. The definition is:

Development that meets the needs of the present without compromising the ability of future generations to meet their own needs. (World Commission on Environment and Development 1987)

It was defined back in 1987 but we've had to wait a few decades before people started 'measuring' wellbeing and human needs.

At the moment there is no published or standard method of quantifying the wellbeing impacts of carbon emissions. Therefore I worked on the following idea. The United Nations High Commission on Refugees reviewed projections on how many environmental refugees might be caused by adverse changes to our climate (UNHCR 2012). There was a wide range of projections but, for this methodology, 200 million environmental refugees by 2050 is used as a near consensus estimate (Gaynor 2020). When I first did the calculations though, the projection was five million refugees.

For example, people in Africa and Bangladesh are leaving

areas where their environment can no longer feed, water or shelter them. With their basic needs denied, they will not be able to pursue higher wellbeing needs. These effects can be linked to climate change.

When I did these calculations a few years ago, OECD figures indicated that in 2010, 3×10^{10} tonnes of carbon were emitted in the world. Linking this to the previous figure of five million refugees, it can be estimated that one environmental refugee is caused for every 6,000 tonnes of carbon emissions.

For the UK, which emits 831 million tonnes of carbon annually (at the time of my calculations), this equates to around 140,000 environmental refugees caused by our emissions. In other words, 140,000 people somewhere in the world are denied maximum wellbeing because of UK emissions. It should be noted that these figures are an oversimplification. However, this is an area for future research and could provide valuable insight into the achievement of maximum wellbeing at a global scale.

Materials impact

In nations such as the UK, we rely on materials for everything from running hospitals to building our homes, agricultural industries and even putting food on our tables. The extraction and processing of materials cause carbon emissions and air, water and land pollution. At times, the supply of these materials can cause armed conflicts in their countries of origin. For these reasons it is important to evaluate the extent to which the way we extract and use materials use is causing illbeing outside our own population. As with other wellbeing impacts, no standard figures are available, so this is a proposed method I developed back in 2014.

A United Nations report indicates that 40 per cent of conflicts arise from access to resources (UNEP 2009). Since 1990 at least 18 violent conflicts have been fuelled by the exploitation of natural resources. Case studies in the report estimate 4.5 million deaths and displacements for every two such conflicts, meaning that in the 19 years between 1990 and 2009, when the report was published, irresponsibly sourced materials were responsible for around 40.5 million deaths and displacements.

So how do we calculate how many resources the world uses? The UK's Defra (a government department with a remit for environmental protection) produced some figures that stated that imports to the UK are 125mt (metric tonnes) per year (see tradingeconomics.com/united-kingdom/gdp). So, that would equate to 2,375mt in the 19 years between 1990 and 2009, when the UN report was published. We know that the UK accounts for roughly 4 per cent of world GDP so, assuming a correlation between a nation's GDP and its use of materials, world imports could equal 59,375mt between 1990 and 2009. So, you could say that these imports caused 40.5 million conflict deaths and displacements. That is, every 1,466 tonnes of imports, unethically sourced, caused a death or displacement (ie an environmental refugee) due to resource conflicts.

In the UK we do recycle many materials and ethically purchase around 8.5 per cent of our imports (the figure in DEFRA 2014 refers to food but I am assuming it roughly holds across other purchases). In addition, the 2014 WWF Living planet report shows that the UK uses roughly 2.3 times its fair share of the planet's resources. Another way of interpreting this is that 43 per cent of our resources are fairly imported. The diagram overleaf shows these figures pictorially (based on the 2014 figure for the UK population of 64.1 million).

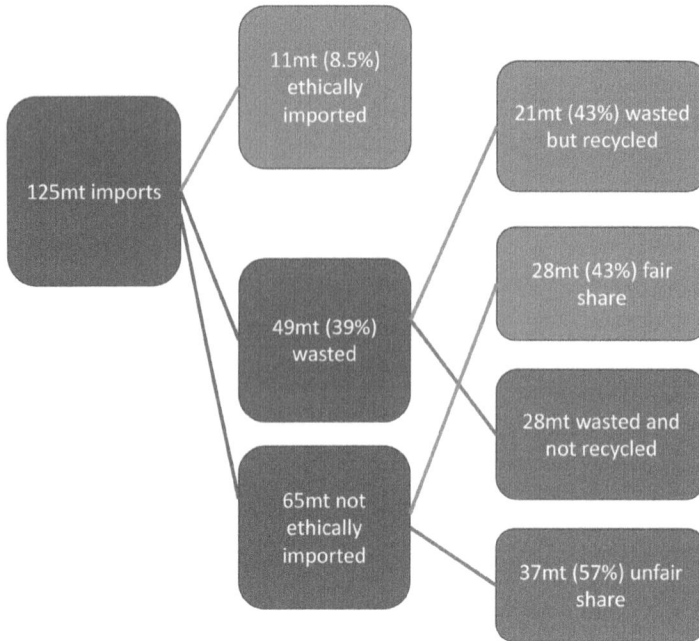

This means that 65mt (28mt + 37mt) is unfairly sourced, which according to our calculations above results in 43,656 environmental refugees.

Yet again, the problem is that we have no established or standard figures for this kind of calculation. So while it is tempting to try to work out the direct impact of our behaviours in the UK on people in other parts of the world, the idea that we can calculate our wellbeing, then subtract the 'illbeing' we cause people in other countries to leave us with a value called 'net wellbeing' is problematic. One thing we do know, however, is that conflicts around the world are driven by resource control, so further research in this area is urgently needed.

In the end, I found that in the developed world our impacts are causing us enough security issues of our own. This will surely be enough of an incentive to reduce our impacts without complicating it with worthy but perhaps less immediate aims of helping someone else.

Utopia?

On holiday one year I was chatting to someone I met about my idea of using Maslow as a framework for measuring wellbeing. I explained this could be a way to manage the world so that 100 per cent of the people on the planet are 100 per cent happy. His response was, 'The problem is, Rich, you want Utopia.' I found this reaction illuminating. I've met with similar responses from other people, especially when it comes to wanting 100 per cent security. Many police officers, for example, say that we'll never achieve 100 per cent security. But yes, I do want Utopia – who wouldn't? I don't see that as a problem.

My view is that we definitely won't achieve Utopia if we are not even aiming for it. I'm glad that new metrics are evolving around wellbeing. Not only does this allow us to monitor our progress but it also allows us to hold our politicians to account. They can go on all day long about budget spends and new strategies but if at the end of the day our wellbeing has decreased, then maybe that's what we should bear in mind at the ballot box.

Chapter 2
Happiness, money and sex

When asked what makes people happy, perhaps Maslow and his hierarchy of needs is not the first thing that comes to mind. Many people might say it's money, power or sex. So where do these things fit into our definition of wellbeing?

Money, money, money

Like it or not, in the UK we live in a capitalist society. We need money to buy stuff; we pay our taxes with money. For some people it serves as a status symbol. Because of this, it is natural for us all to think about money from time to time – wishing we had more, admiring what others do with theirs and wondering what we would do if we won the lottery. Some of us believe that the entire world is motivated by money and greed and that most of what businesses and governments do is purely to line their coffers. Furthermore, we believe this is the natural state of affairs.

It isn't. Money is a man-made social construct. To see this, and to understand how relatively recently we have operated in a monetary society, it might be useful to look at how money came about. Initially, physical money was a token of value and everyone who used it trusted that the token had that value (Bank of England 2020). This money wasn't coins but other items such as shells, teeth and sacks of grain.

Eventually these tokens of money started to be made from metals such as silver and gold. These metals were particularly favoured because they were long lasting and rare enough to be valuable. At some point in our history, jewellers were asked by people who held gold or silver coins to store those coins safely. The person would deposit their coins with the jeweller, who in return would write the equivalent of an IOU note. Whoever held that IOU note could then trade it in for the amount of gold written on it. This meant that the IOU notes themselves had value. And because they were easier to carry around, more and more trade was done on the basis of exchanging IOU notes for goods or services. If whoever held the IOU note needed actual gold coins, they could go back to the jeweller and claim their gold. These jewellers eventually evolved into what we now call banks and IOU notes became banknotes.

Up until 1931 banknotes could be exchanged for gold held in central reserves. One of the constraints of this system was that any economic development was limited to how much gold could be mined. But after 1931 banknotes were issued as a fiat currency – that is, one that cannot be converted into any physical asset held by central banks. Today, around 96 per cent of all money held in your bank account is electronic and not cash. The other 4 per cent is backed up with banknotes and coins. So the whole system is run on trust in the fiat currency.

This system opens the door for the invention of new currencies. In theory, if you can get enough people to trust in the currency, then you can use it for trading. An example of this from the past few years is Bitcoin. This cryptocurrency has gained trust among some users and hence has become established in some circles as a viable currency. One of the attractions of Bitcoin is that it is not controlled by central banks. It is based on trust, in that it uses so-called distributed ledger technology called blockchain to trace all transactions that a single electronic Bitcoin has been through. This means that Bitcoin cannot be forged because the forged coins wouldn't have the right ledger transactions. Here are some ways you can gain Bitcoins:

1. Sell goods or services for Bitcoins.

2. Buy Bitcoins with more established currency.

3. Mine Bitcoin. This is where you use lots of computer power to solve puzzles. The puzzle solving isn't really the point though – the point is to use the computers that are doing the puzzles to keep a record of the transactions, ie they are part of the distributed ledger that helps maintain the trust in the currency. As a reward for using your computers you get paid in Bitcoins. In other words, you've 'mined' them. The puzzles are made easier or harder to help control the flow of Bitcoins.

Other currencies come and go. Local currencies (eg the Brixton pound featuring David Bowie on its B£20 note) are intended to keep money in the local economy. And there are other schemes that use time as the currency. For example, one person may walk another person's dog for an hour and gain an hour of time owed to them. Someone else in that scheme may then do an hour of babysitting and get paid that banked hour. The organisation Timebanking provides great resources for time exchange schemes through the UK (timebanking.org).

But currency of any kind only works when it is distributed fairly. I used to be part of a babysitting circle that used tokens to track who had babysat and for how long. You earned tokens for hours of babysitting and you were then able to pay these tokens to other babysitters in the group when you wanted a babysitter. Once a month the number of tokens in circulation was tracked (ie a ledger). But after a while the system started to break down because one person in the group just seemed to want to collect the tokens. They were keen to earn tokens by doing lots of babysitting but they didn't seem to want to go out and therefore didn't require anyone in the group to babysit for them. This meant that they eventually accumulated all the tokens in circulation.

The result was one person with a wealth of tokens but presumably they were not that happy because they weren't going out and having fun. And the rest of us were unhappy because we didn't have any tokens left because they were all held by the 'wealthy' person. This led me to question why on earth that person was in the group at all if they had no intention of requiring a babysitter. This was probably one of the best lessons in economics I've ever had. It seemed that, conversely to what we might think, *acquiring* money didn't increase wellbeing if that meant that the money was not evenly distributed to the rest of the group. The more uneven the wealth, the lower the overall wellbeing.

Maslow tokens

I wonder what it would be like if we had a new currency based on wellbeing? In exchange for doing something good for the wellbeing of yourself or someone else you could earn 'Maslow tokens' from the beneficiary of that good deed. That way, people who just wanted to accumulate wealth for the sake of it could carry on doing it but their wealth would represent how much good they did for the rest of the people on the planet.

For now we are stuck with pounds and pence, the value of which is determined, ultimately, by political will, which may or may not be directed towards the wellbeing of everyone. Certainly a lot of focus in the UK is given to improving the economy and job creation. The assumption seems to be that the wealth created from this will trickle down to everyone. Much has been written on whether the trickle-down effect really works or whether it has to be managed, through taxes or other ways of clawing it back from those who have accumulated it and are not using it.

In the end in the babysitting circle we had to place a time limit on how long the tokens could be held before they had to be returned to the pot. This allowed us to extract the tokens from the individual who had accumulated them so that the system continued to work and we could all be happy. I guess the person who had all their tokens taken may not have immediately seen it that way, though.

Let's talk about sex

Clearly sex is a human need. If it wasn't then there would be no little humans around. Sex appears in different sections of Maslow's hierarchy depending on which source you read. In some it is classed as one of our basic needs, described as reproduction; in others it is a security need (as a health need) and in others still it appears in the social section as a need for intimacy. Where it actually sits in the hierarchy is probably dependent on an individual's point of view but the point is, it's in there.

For better or worse British people don't talk about sex. That said, there have been some studies on the subject and how it affects our wellbeing. Here are the results of one study on sexual activity and subjective wellbeing using data from about 4,000 English people over the age of 50 who have partners (Lee et al. 2016). The researchers classified the people according to low, medium or high levels of desire, intercourse, fondling, masturbation, erectile function, arousal and orgasm. Then they compared the subjective wellbeing of the different classes of people. The study showed that men with low levels of sexual behaviour had 2.57 fewer wellbeing points than men with high sexual behaviour, even taking into account age, health, educational level and closeness to their partner. For women the corresponding figure was 1.35.

The study also concluded that:

- ⮝ men with low partnered sexual activity but who masturbated frequently had lower life satisfaction but this difference became nonsignificant when closeness to their partner was considered

- ⮝ women who frequently engaged in partnered sex and had few functional difficulties had higher life satisfaction

- ⮝ women who had low desire but engaged in partnered sex regularly saw no significant change to their life satisfaction as long as they had closeness to their partner

- ⮝ higher levels on a depression scoring metric were recorded for men and women with low levels of sexual activity but the differences were insignificant if there was high closeness to their partner.

What studies like this show is that it is possible to a) measure happiness and b) identify which factors do and do not contribute to greater wellbeing. Sometimes they show that our assumptions about what makes us happy are in fact wrong.

Chapter 3
Safe as houses?

The first two levels of Maslow's hierarchy are physical and biological facts. No amount of personal feelings about how happy we are can change the physical reality of the environment in which we live. You can't 'happy' yourself out of starvation for any sustained period. Humans need food and food security but also clean drinking water, clean air and warmth. Helpfully, the NHS has quantified what is sufficient to satisfy these needs: for example, 2,500 calories of food a day for men and 2,000 for women (see nhs.uk/common-health-questions/food-and-diet/what-should-my-daily-intake-of-calories-be) and a certain level of air quality. Without satisfying these basic needs, humans will not survive, let alone achieve wellbeing.

Basically OK

We can assume that in the UK our basic needs are met. Most of us have food, water, thermal comfort and air, regardless of background. Or do we? Even in the UK, there are cases of people dying because their basic needs have not been met. Here are some statistics for each year in the UK:

- about 28,000 excess winter deaths due to cold weather (before Covid-19 – see ONS 2020)

⬤ about 2,000 excess deaths due to heatwaves (UKHSA 2022)

⬤ about 36,000 premature deaths due to poor air quality (Public Health England 2019).

Any built environment should be developed to ensure that, at the very least, these needs are met, for example by having housing that is warm in cold weather and cool in warmer weather and allowing for adequate distribution of food, water and sanitation.

A major contributor to winter deaths is fuel poverty (BEIS 2016). In 2022 this became a real issue and has led to severe thermal comfort problems for millions of people in the UK. Major contributing factors to fuel poverty are energy-inefficient housing and low levels of income.

However, as tragic as these circumstances are, given the nearly 70 million population of the UK, these deaths represent around 0.1 per cent. So in Maslow speak, around 99.9 per cent of our basic needs are met in the UK and that is the assumption we will make for the purposes of this book. So for the box on page vii, we can say that in the UK we score 50 out of 50 for our basic needs being met as a nation. In other countries, this may not be the case. For instance, countries at war, suffering from disease epidemics or from recent natural disasters will have many more people whose basic needs are not being met. We'll look more at metrics for food supply later on in the section 'What's for dinner?'.

If a framework such as Maslow's was used to measure our success as a nation, then we should surely prioritise work to ensure these basic needs are met for 100 per cent of the population. In the rest of this chapter I aim to quantify how secure we currently are in the UK in the widest sense.

Security

Having looked at deaths, now I will outline the lack of security of supply of our basic needs due to environmental factors. As bad as all that is, these sections are not meant to be doom-mongering. Most of us have a lot to be thankful for but there is room for improvement.

The data is there to give us an honest appraisal of where we are right now. What's more, we can see what 'good' looks like and give ourselves a gap analysis. Once we see the gaps, we can start to take action to fill them. This book is about how individuals can do their bit to fill those gaps but there is a role for government in all this too.

According to Maslow, once we have satisfied our basic needs, we seek to satisfy security needs. On one level, this may be security from physical attack, either home grown or from outside our built environments. For most of us, perhaps more pressing is the security of supply of our basic needs like food, water, thermal comfort and air. In other words, it's not enough that we have these things right now; we need to know that we will have them in the future, too.

Quantifying security is notoriously difficult. After all, we don't really know we are insecure until something happens. When nothing bad happens we tend to feel secure. And if we feel secure, why spend time or money on improving our security? Why not spend that money on fun things like holidays? And when something really bad happens we are often plunged back into trying to sort out our basic immediate needs rather than worry about our security. This can happen at a national level too. For example, when crime rates fall, governments decide to cut police spending.

This is often the case with things we can't see. For example, CO_2 emissions are colourless, odourless emissions but when they enter our atmosphere in too high a concentration, they cause catastrophic impacts. In this chapter we will see that our environmental impacts are already affecting our security, and how we can define security in a metric so we can see what 'good' looks like in numbers. The aim is to achieve 100 per cent security for the rest of our lives.

Floody hell

One of the UK's Met Office climate change projections for the UK is more frequent incidences of high intensity rainfall events. Depending on which forecasting model they use and what may or may not happen to humanity's level of carbon emissions, the amount of extra winter rainfall compared to 1981–2010 averages can vary:

- In the case where we dramatically reduce carbon emissions, all of the UK can expect to see around 10 per cent more winter rain.

- If emissions carry on growing at the current rate some parts of Scotland could get 30 per cent more rain.

- Where emissions carry on growing at the current rate some parts of south-east England will get 10 per cent more rainfall.

You can look up what climate change may mean for your postcode here: bbc.co.uk/news/resources/idt-d6338d9f-8789-4bc2-b6d7-3691c0e7d138

Hydrologists can input this data into their computer models of river basins to give statistics on the risk of flooding in any particular area. The models are highly sophisticated and use complex statistical analysis. In fact, hydrologists who understand statistical methods for using limited historical data and uncertain futures are sought after by banks and investors to try and predict economic outcomes.

As well as Met Office projections, the hydrologists' models take into account:

- the area of hard paved surfaces that doesn't allow rainwater to permeate into the soil

- the area of green spaces that can allow rainwater to permeate into the soil

- woodland, which delays or attenuates rainwater from reaching the soil

- the amount of water storage, even including puddles

- the dimensions of rivers

- different soil types.

The models then give an idea of flood risk for everywhere in the UK. There are essentially two types of flood risk assessed: fluvial and surface water. Fluvial flood risk is what we may traditionally view as flooding. In other words, so much water floods down a river that it simply doesn't have the capacity to deal with it and it burst its banks. Any properties, towns and villages in the surrounding areas will be flooded.

Surface water is a less traditional view of flooding but is on the rise. We have paved so much of the land where we live and reduced the extent of green spaces that, coupled with the projected higher frequency of intense rainfall events, our existing systems simply cannot deal with the amount of rain and will flood our streets and homes.

But as well as fluvial and surface water flooding there is another form of flood event. Due to climate change we predict higher sea levels, which will bring threats to our shores. The Met Office does not project more tidal surges, though, which are related to atmospheric conditions and not climate. These can lead to coastal erosion as well as coastal flooding.

According to the UK's Environment Agency around one in six homes in the UK (about 17 per cent) are at risk of some form of flooding. It spends millions on flood defence works. But again, when homes do not get flooded people start to question if this money is justified – until a flood event happens, of course. (Try playing the Stop Disasters! Game at stopdisastersgame.org/stop_ disasters for a flavour of these challenges.)

In our consultancy we work with clients to help them discover their flood risk and one group of clients is social housing landlords. If they haven't done it already, we ask them to look at the flood risk of the homes they manage. Here is some data from a range of landlords. Each bar represents an individual landlord and the percentage of the homes they manage which are at low risk of flooding. Some have found that only 10 per cent of the homes are at low risk – but this means that 90 per cent are at some sort of risk! Some have found that nearly all the homes are at low risk. In general though, the findings are similar to the Environment Agency's report.

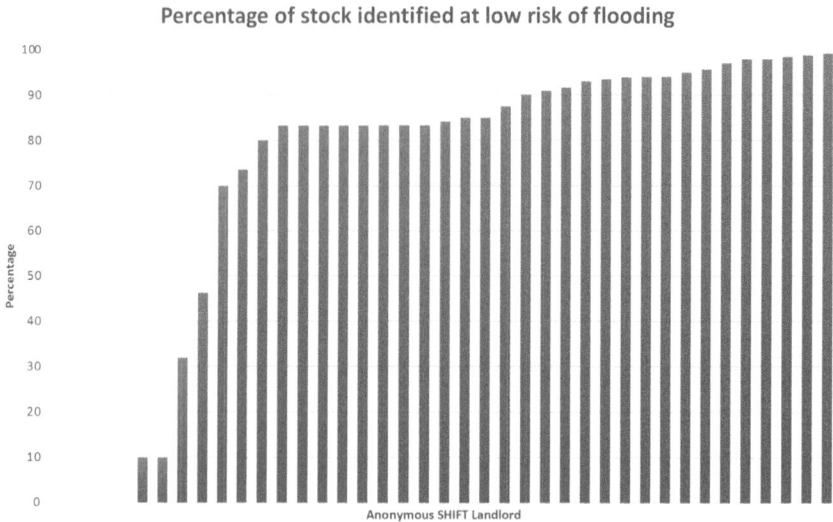

Percentage of stock identified at low risk of flooding

Improving security against flooding increases wellbeing, not just of the tenants of the houses but of the landlords themselves. Flood events create a lot of mess and in some cases raw sewage can enter the home, making it uninhabitable for some considerable time.

You can look up the flood risk of where you live online by typing in your postcode at gov.uk/check-long-term-flood-risk. Be sure to look for fluvial, surface water and coastal flood risks. Each home will be categorised as low, medium or high risk. Note there is no category called 'no risk'. Also note that some homes may be in a high or medium risk area but are protected by an existing artificially built flood barrier.

For our scoring matrix we can say the average UK low flood risk is five out of six homes, ie 83.3 per cent are secure from flooding.

What's for dinner?

Apart from shortages of pasta, tinned tomatoes and flour during the Covid-19 pandemic, in the UK we are pretty well off for food. The supermarket shelves are bulging, farmers' markets are everywhere and takeaways provide us with special treats. In fact, we are also familiar with quite the opposite problem of too much food, as we can see by the obesity rate in the UK. So does this familiarity with plentiful food supplies give us cause for concern? Apart from the occasional panic buy it's not really talked about. But many years ago I was on the island of Barra in the Outer Hebrides and was speaking to a resident about island life. She said that sometimes rumours would go around that there would be a shortage of something like milk. This would start a panic buying spree and pretty soon hoarders would hoover up all the milk in the supermarkets. So the prediction of shortages became a self-fulfilling prophesy.

Panic buying isn't a recent phenomenon. I recall reading an article in *National Geographic* magazine about an archaeologist who decided to investigate landfill sites. One of the unique features of landfill sites is that domestic waste is deposited in layers and each layer is covered with soil or other separating material. The archaeologist investigated waste from the 1970s. He was able to find newspapers from each layer, which enabled him to date that layer very specifically. One finding that puzzled him for a while was that in one layer all the newspaper headlines were describing a lettuce shortage, yet the layer was also full of waste lettuce. Eventually he realised that the news had fuelled panic buying of lettuce and people simply couldn't consume the amount of lettuce they bought and ended up throwing it away. Panic buying aside, for most people in the UK the lack of food security is not caused by threat to our supply but by poor money distribution.

But how could damage to the environment impact our food supplies? Here are a few examples:

- less rainwater, leading to droughts and the inability to irrigate crops
- storms destroying crops
- storms preventing the food we buy from other countries from getting to their destination
- new weather patterns bringing in new pests quicker than local crops can adapt to them.

The last one has affected my own potato crop in our garden, which regularly succumbs to potato blight. This disease is becoming more prevalent now because climate change has made our weather warmer, providing a nice environment in which the fungus-like potato blight micro-organism can survive.

With all these threats to our food supply, it seems that it is more essential than ever to know where we stand on food security in this country. Alas, there are no government figures to monitor this but there are plenty of reports that talk about it.

There is one dataset that can provide us with an indication. *The Economist* has a business unit that produces a Global Food Security Index. For each country, the index amasses good-quality data (usually United Nations sources). They look at a range of issues, such as food prices, food quality, distribution and political corruption levels. In recent years they have been including environmental impacts. Each bundle of factors is input into an algorithm that generates the index score, which is essentially marks out of 100 for each country. At the time of writing, the UK's overall score is 81 out of 100. The scores for the four main subcategories are:

- affordability
- availability
- quality and safety
- natural resources and resilience.

And here's how we compare to a selection of other countries:

- USA – 79.1
- Denmark – 76.5
- Germany – 78.7
- China – 71.3
- India – 57.2
- Kenya – 46.8.

Eighty-one out of 100 may not sound that bad. If I had scored that in my English test at school I would have been elated. But if we take the figure literally it could mean that, unless things improve, in the future for 81 days out of 100 there might be food, and for 19 days out of 100 there might be no food. We could be faced with looking at our kids and asking them on which day out of the next five do they not want to eat.

In terms of metrics, using this index we could say that we are currently 81 per cent food secure. But clearly we need to be 100 per cent secure, and as we can see from the list of weather events above, a huge part of the gap between where we are now and where we should be is environmental damage.

In 2021 the UK national food strategy was released (nationalfoodstrategy.org). It was the sugar and salt taxes in the strategy that made the headlines, but the original brief for the author was to review the entire food system. Many of the resultant recommendations related to environmental protection. For example, the strategy recognises the contribution that agriculture makes to UK greenhouse gas emissions (eg methane from cows, fertiliser degradation) and biodiversity (habitat destruction, pollution), but it also recognises that the damage we do to our environment may well impact on crop yields and other aspects of food production and supply.

To combat the adverse environmental parts of our food system the strategy makes some key recommendations:

- ⋏ Support farmers to make a transition to sustainable practices. This ensures an income is available to farmers that makes it viable for them to grow our food by paying them for environmental stewardship. The stewardship will take the form of carbon sequestration and habitat creation.

- ⋏ Develop a rural land use framework and map that directs policy towards efficient use of land from an environmental perspective (eg forestry, energy crops, peatland or agroforestry). The strategy notes that around 2.2 per cent of total UK land will be needed for new housing by 2060.

- ⋏ Require public bodies (schools, prisons, hospitals etc) to buy sustainable food. The public sector spends around £2.4 billion per year and this huge wedge of taxpayers' money can be used for good and have a knock-on effect for other sectors.

- ⋏ Introduce environmental impact labelling to allow consumers to make more informed purchasing choices.

The 'food security' chapter of the strategy highlights that, at the moment, food production contributes to environmental degradation. In turn this 'will decrease crop yields, which could lead to higher prices and make societies more vulnerable to famine, food riots and conflict'. While the strategy doesn't specifically mention a metric for monitoring our food security, following the adage that you can only manage what you measure, it would make sense to have one that includes environmental issues. Until a metric is developed, the *Economist*'s Global Food Security Index could be a good surrogate (foodsecurityindex.eiu.com). A big chunk of why we are not 100 per cent food secure is down to a poor score on 'natural resources and resilience'.

Environmental protection is a crucial factor in securing the supply of all our basic needs. As well as food, clean air and water, even our own homes are at risk if we fail to act. The starting point is an environmental baseline, together with an idea of what 'good' looks like.

Phew, what a scorcher!

Another of the UK Met Office's projections for our future weather relates to how much warmer our summers will become. The central projection is 2°C warmer average summer temperatures but again this can vary widely depending on what will happen with future carbon emissions, where in the country you are and which output of the computer modelling you look at. Here are some of the variations:

- ⋏ Assuming a massive reduction in carbon emissions, Scotland will have no change in summer temperature, whereas south-east England can expect a 1–2°C increase.

- ⋏ Assuming a central projection of carbon reductions, average summer temperatures in Scotland could rise by about 1°C, and in south-east England it could be 2°C.

- ⋏ In the worst-case scenario, where carbon emissions continue unabated, average summer temperatures Scotland could expect a 1–2°C increase and the south-east of England will increase by 2–3°C.

It takes a bit of playing around but you can examine the relevant maps here: ukclimateprojections-ui.metoffice.gov.uk/products (free login required)

The thought of our summers getting warmer might sound nice. We can imagine more time sitting in the sun and enjoying life. But an average summer temperature increase of 2°C masks the fact that on individual days, temperatures can soar much higher than that and give us heatwaves. In the wrong type of house heatwaves can make internal temperatures unbearable. And if the heatwave persists for more than a few days with no chance to cool down this can lead to serious health problems. In recent heatwaves in the UK, excess summer deaths are recorded as 2,556, which is comparable to the 2003 heatwave (Public Health England 2020). There is ongoing research to see if Covid had any amplifying effect on summer deaths. In 2022 new record summer temperatures were recorded for the UK.

There are a range of risk factors that will affect whether a home will overheat:

- ⋏ **When the home was built.** New homes have been built according to building regulations designed to keep warmth in with the aim of conserving energy in the home. This has led to reasonably well-insulated homes. It has also led to homes being increasingly airtight. This airtightness is achieved by sealing up any gaps that are a feature of older homes, for instance when a pipe is cut through a wall or where the roof sits on the walls. An air permeability test was introduced in recent building regulations which ensures that air leakage rate from a home should be less than 10 m^3/m^2/hr. Typical new-builds achieve an air leakage rate of 4–5 m^3/m^2/hr, which means there is little natural ventilation.

Good for keeping the warm air in during winter but bad for letting warm air out in summer.

⌄ **Where the home is.** A 2°C average summer temperature rise in south-east England will have a greater impact than a 2°C rise in Scotland where summer temperatures are typically much cooler. That's not to say that overheating can't occur in Scotland (it can), because there are other risk factors.

⌄ **Urban heat islands.** If the home is located in an area with a high density of dwellings, with lots of concrete, tarmac and other mineral-based materials, then there is an increased risk of overheating. During heatwaves, these materials absorb the heat during the day and then during the supposedly cooler evening they radiate it back out to the surrounding area.

⌄ **Type of home.** Flats and apartments typically have fewer external walls, floors and roofs from which to radiate their excess heat. This is great for winter warmth but bad for summer heat.

⌄ **Ventilation levels.** This has never been a huge focus for our buildings and is particularly hard to assess. But if the home has poor ventilation capability, this is a risk factor because there is no means to exhaust excess heat. A particularly poor example of design is that of so-called 'single aspect' homes. These are homes where windows can only be opened on one side of the home. This ensures that no cross ventilation can occur because there is no flow route for the air. Sadly, this is typical for flats and apartments. You might be lucky and have the home built by a conscientious builder who has thought about good ventilation but all too often this is a key risk factor.

⅄ **Type of heating.** This again typically affects flats and apartments. If there is communal heating (eg a boiler in the basement feeding hot water and warmth to the flats above) then typically the heat is transferred via pipes that run along corridors. These pipes may be poorly insulated, causing heat to leak into corridors and then through walls and doors exposed to these corridors.

Overheating is a growing problem, with some new-build homes recording internal temperatures in excess of 50°C. On top of this, our building regulations as far as overheating is concerned are severely lacking. The calculations involved are poorly regulated and even if they were well regulated, the current methodologies take no account of projected summer temperatures nor the impacts of communal heating systems.

So how secure are we from overheating? Sadly, the answer is that no one knows. Despite the potential problems above, there is no central monitoring of the risk. A now-defunct quango-like organisation called Zero Carbon Hub estimated that about 20 per cent of homes are at risk of overheating but the reality is that no one really knows.

In our consultancy work with UK social landlords we developed a tool at SHIFT Environment to allow landlords to assess the number of risk factors in the homes they manage. From our analysis, we think that homes that have one or two risk factors are at low risk of overheating. Three to four risk factors would have medium risk and five or six risk factors would be high risk. From the data we have, which may (or may not) be representative of all tenures, our analysis finds that 79 per cent of homes are at low risk of overheating, which is similar to the Zero Carbon Hub report.

In Chapter 6 I'll describe how a simple tweak in the way we assess the energy efficiency of our homes could allow us to get a much better national handle on this.

The grass is always greener

Green spaces and biodiversity have suffered hugely in the UK. Here are some sobering statistics from a recent report (State of Nature Partnership 2019):

- ↟ The indicator for 696 terrestrial and freshwater species shows a significant decline of 13 per cent in average abundance since 1970 and has fallen by 6 per cent over the past 10 years.

- ↟ Since 1970, 41 per cent of species have decreased in abundance.

- ↟ Over the past 10 years, 44 per cent of species have decreased.

- ↟ Long-term decreases in average abundance in butterflies since 1976 (16 per cent) and moths since 1970 (25 per cent) have not slowed.

- ↟ The mammal indicator shows little change since 1994.

- ↟ There have been declines in common and widespread breeding species of birds.

- ↟ The total number of breeding birds in the UK fell by 44 million between 1967 and 2009.

While this all sounds very sad, it's less easy to see the direct connection between the loss of our green spaces and biodiversity and the immediate impacts upon us in terms of supply of our basic needs. But here are some examples (overleaf):

Element of biodiversity	Benefit
Bees	Bees play a crucial role in pollinating the crops we eat. Without suitable habitats for bees we won't have them and we won't have crops.
Trees and other vegetation	The more vegetation that grows, the more benefits we accrue as humans. For our consultancy work we use a blunt metric called 'above ground biomass' – in other words, matter that grows above the ground. It doesn't capture all issues relating to biodiversity but it does give a pretty good surrogate measure (see below). It shows that having high levels of plants growing above ground does correlate with better air cleaning, better flood attenuation and better summer cooling during heatwaves. This correlates with higher levels of biodiversity, which correlates with higher levels of carbon sequestration, which is generally good for climate change. There are also other security benefits.
'Early warning' animals	For example, rats moving away from certain areas just prior to an earthquake (see Shadbolt 2015).
Diversity	There are more than 30,000 different plant species with a known human use, but globally we obtain more than half our calories from just three species (wheat, rice and maize). If a disease affected those three, we'd be in trouble.
Biomimicry – this is where biodiverse habitats are studied to learn things that are beneficial for humans.	Examples include efficient air conditioning designs based on termite mounds and the discovery of medicines derived from plants.
Biodiverse open spaces	Open spaces provide areas for recreation and even study, so that social, esteem and self-actualisation needs can be satisfied.

Given the benefits of biodiversity for satisfying human needs, it is clearly critical that we protect it. And if we want to protect or enhance biodiversity then we need to be able to measure it. At the time of writing, the measurement of so-called natural capital is in its infancy. A UK government group called the Natural Capital Committee has developed a proposed method. Interestingly, one of the first stages of the method is to assess the human benefits that a particular biodiverse region satisfies. However, the Natural Capital methodology converts nature into pounds and pence, so is not ideal to indicate how secure our biodiversity is. But we can get some clues from various government reports and policies, which we can assume are based on the relevant science. Here's an overview of the policies:

Country	Existing woodland (ha)	Additional woodland target (ha)	Target date	% increase in wood-land	Source
England	1,320,000	180,000	2043	13.6	Woodland Statistics 2021 – Forestry Commission A Green Future: Our 25 Year Plan to Improve the Environment – UK government
Wales	310,000	100,000	2030	32.3	Woodland Statistics 2021 – Forestry Commission Woodland Creation Report Wales - Research Agency of the Forestry Commission
Scotland	1,480,000	173,200	2032	11.7	Woodland Statistics 2021 – Forestry Commission Scotland's Forestry Strategy 2019 - 2029 – Scottish Government

The nearly 15 per cent necessary increase needed indicates that we only have 85 per cent of the necessary amount of woodland, ie we are not 100 per cent secure on this. Woodland isn't necessarily the same as biodiversity, particularly if you think of monoculture pine forests in Scotland, which are just grown for wood production. However, according to the now-defunct Code for Sustainable Homes, the average number of plant species per hectare generally increases as a piece of land is more wooded.

Water, water, everywhere?

Water is an essential human need. We simply cannot live without it. It's necessary for maintaining fluid levels in our bodies and is also critical for sanitation. In the UK we are used to complaining about the rain and it's been a long time since we had water shortages, although they have happened in our past. In fact, flooding is now so much more common that it feels unnatural to talk about water shortages. Nevertheless, the Met Office climate projections suggest that by 2050 there could be up to 10 per cent less annual rainfall and up to 20 per cent less summer rainfall based on central projections alone. If things got really bad (ie carbon emissions continued to increase and the worst-case scenarios in the climate models are realised) this could get as bad as 50 per cent less in some parts of the country.

The Environment Agency (2009) looked at climate projections, coupled with population increase projections. They also looked at water usage for agriculture and industry. Essentially, they found that we will have to share less annual rainwater with more people. They concluded that domestic water efficiency should be 130 litres per person per day but that at the time they did their research, in some areas of the UK water usage was 170 litres per person per day. In 2021 the average water use in the UK was 142 litres per person per day (see discoverwater.co.uk/amount-we-use). So when we turn this into a percentage, we can see that we are only 92 per cent secure for water in the future.

It might be helpful to think about what 142 litres per person per day looks like. Here are some facts to take into consideration:

- a standard bath filled to the overflow is around 160 litres
- an old-style cistern toilet flush is around 15 litres of water per flush
- when disaster relief organisations plan water sourcing for refugees they plan on 70 litres per person per day
- soldiers are assumed to drink six litres of water a day
- cross-Atlantic sailors are advised to ration 4.5 litres per crew member per day for the crossing.

I met a sailor who had crossed the Atlantic using that rationing but he was so careful with water consumption that he had plenty left when he got to the other side. He calculated that he had used only 2.5 litres per day by using seawater for bathing and cooking pasta and potatoes.

So achieving 130 litres per person per day doesn't sound like that much of an imposition and we as humans can easily adapt to using that amount. Another advantage of water efficiency applies particularly when you save hot water, as not only are you saving the water but you are also emitting less carbon because you haven't heated it.

Water companies also use a lot of carbon-emitting energy to pump water around our systems. The last time I calculated this for individual households it did not represent a huge carbon saving for the home (around 12kgs CO_2 per year for pumping our water compared to 4 tonnes CO_2 associated with heating and hot water for the average home). That said, if you save hot water, it starts to make a much bigger difference.

Financial security

Despite the discussion on money in Chapter 2, at present we live in a capitalist economy. We need money to satisfy our needs: both basic ones, like homes and food, and non-basic, like fun. So, any measure of security should include how financially secure we are. This is not the same as maximising the amount of money we have. Not everyone strives for this and many are perfectly happy with enough money. Ideally, we should have enough money to cover our daily needs, a little in reserve for those unexpected surprises and perhaps a pension fund so we can look after ourselves in later years. According to the Money and Pensions Service (MaPS), financial wellbeing is 'about feeling secure and in control of your finances, both now and in the future' (moneyandpensionsservice.org.uk/what-is-financial-wellbeing). It's knowing that you can pay the bills today, can deal with the unexpected and are on track for a healthy financial future. The ONS and MaPS have some statistics on this (ONS 2021, 2022):

- 14 per cent of people find debt a 'heavy burden', 30 per cent 'somewhat of a burden' and 57 per cent 'not a problem at all'

- 77.6 per cent of us had some kind of pension in 2020 – this shot up from 46.5 per cent in 2012 just before auto-enrolment into pension schemes was introduced

- 11.5 million people had less than £100 in savings to fall back on

- 9 million people often borrowed to buy food or pay bills

- 22 million people said they don't know enough to plan for their retirement

- 5.3 million children didn't get a meaningful financial education.

Sadly, there isn't a single figure of how many of us are financially secure or otherwise, but these statistics do portray a grim reality that it's way off 100 per cent. By taking the top two figures, ie 57 per cent find debt no problem and 77.6 per cent of us have a pension, we can take an average of 67.3 per cent, which we can use for our UK figure of financial security.

Crime, fun and CO$_2$

I once delivered a talk at an event hosted by comedian Marcus Brigstocke to outline my Maslow proposals. On seeing this slide, Marcus commented that he'd never thought he'd see a slide entitled 'Crime, fun and CO$_2$'. But the concept is important. We've seen that environmental security is vital for our long-term wellbeing and that we must reduce our environmental impacts to ensure a secure future. However, there are other security issues not directly related to environmental protection.

Again, we have no single figure to measure our physical security. The best we can do is to look at current crime rates and derive a percentage security level from that. Here's what we know from the ONS Crime Survey from year ending 2021 (ONS 2017, 2021b, 2022b):

- During the Covid-19 lockdowns crime (except for fraud) decreased but then rebounded.

- 13.6 per cent of us were victims of some form of crime, including fraud from telephone surveys.

- Actual recorded 'victim-based' (ie some kind of personal attack) crime was 67 incidents per 1,000 people, or 6.7 per cent.

- We don't have a figure for fear of crime, but in the last figures for this in 2016 this was measured at 19 per cent. This was derived from the number of respondents who reported a perceived likelihood of victimisation, answering 'very likely' or 'fairly likely'. The figure was slightly higher for women than men.

The interesting thing is that often the perception of crime appears to be higher than the number of actual recorded incidents.

It is difficult to know whether this is due to a lack of incidents being recorded or to excess anxiety about crime, but it's clear there is a difference. Assuming the actual recorded victim-based crime figures are accurate, ie 67 per 1,000, that means that 933 people per 1,000 *weren't* victims of crime, which gives us a figure of 93.3 per cent security from victim-based crime.

A great fear in the past few decades has been terrorism, and we can use the assessment of the risk of a terror attack to help us with our model for predicting overall security. The different levels of threat have changed over the years but the current set is:

- ▲ **low** means an attack is highly unlikely
- ▲ **moderate** means an attack is possible but not likely
- ▲ **substantial** means an attack is likely
- ▲ **severe** means an attack is highly likely
- ▲ **critical** means an attack is highly likely in the near future.

At the time of writing, we are at 'substantial' level (mi5.gov.uk/threat-levels). But can we change this into a number? One method would be to assign a score to each level and to measure how long we were at that level over the past year. For example, if we were at low risk of an attack for the past 12 months, this would score 100 per cent, but if we were at critical for the past 12 months, this would score 0 per cent. Moderate would be 75 per cent, substantial would be 50 per cent and severe would be 25 per cent. Here's some recent history at the time of writing:

Date	National Threat Level
15 November 2021	SEVERE
4 February 2021	SUBSTANTIAL
3 November 2020	SEVERE
4 November 2019	SUBSTANTIAL
23 July 2019	SEVERE

From 15 November 2020 to 14 November 2021 the UK spent 284 days at substantial risk and 81 days at severe risk. Using the scoring mechanism above, 284 days x 50 per cent substantial + 84 days x 25 per cent divided by 365 days would translate as people in the UK being 44 per cent secure over the past year.

You give me fever

The Covid-19 pandemic has alerted us to how vulnerable we are as human beings to disease. The 2018 UK Biological Security Strategy (HM Government 2018) noted:

The risk of high impact infectious disease is constantly changing. The continuing global trends of migration towards urban centres, and the expansion of international travel, increase the potential for diseases to spread. Other drivers such as changes in diets in urban populations and the rapidly rising demand for animal-sourced foods will increase the interactions between humans, domestic livestock and wildlife, changing the nature of the risk of new zoonotic outbreaks.

Alas, there is no percentage security figure for biological threats. However, if there were, we would be in a better position to not only manage this serious threat to our wellbeing but also to hold our politicians to account.

In response to the Covid-19 pandemic, in June 2021 the government published a 100-day mission to respond to future pandemics (Pandemic Preparedness Partnership 2021). There is an interesting comment in the document which highlights that there was a 'historical reduction in financing that is seen once health threats have diminished'. In other words, once the perceived threat of global pandemic diminishes, funding for contingency plans also wanes. The 100-day mission's plan is to detect diseases of concern early and make vaccine production financially viable. However, there is no mention of a numerical biological security rating.

Summary of security by numbers

Combining the security percentages we've looked at in this chapter into one figure, we can fill out this box:

Issue	% secure
Flood risk	83.3%
Food security	78.5%
Overheating	79.0%
Biodiversity	85.0%
Water security	92.0%
Financial security	67.3%
Crime	93.3%
Average	82.6%

To put this figure into the scoring matrix on page vii, we need to convert it to a score out of 25, which we can do simply by multiplying by 0.25. So the answer we get for how secure we are is 20.7 out of 25.

So, as we start to build a picture of our overall wellbeing according to the Maslow scale, how happy are we on a basic level? We assume that our basic requirements are catered for but we also know that even here in the UK there is a lack of security for our most essential needs. Flooding, overheating and food insecurity all threaten our long-term wellbeing. This is, ironically, largely due to our own impacts on the environment around us. The threats from crime, terrorism and pandemic similarly loom large, undermining our aimed-for 100 per cent wellbeing score.

But what about our more complex needs as we climb the Maslow hierarchy? How happy are we on a social and personal level?

Chapter 4
Happy now?

Once we've covered our basic needs and security, how do we know how happy we are on a social, esteem and self-actualisation level? As difficult as our physical wellbeing is to measure, surely it is even more challenging to calculate our emotional and social happiness? Not necessarily so. As we saw in Chapter 1, it turns out that simply asking people to mark themselves out of 10 as to how they feel is more telling than you might think. In the Action for Happiness report (see Chapter 1), for example, people's own judgement of their life satisfaction correlated pretty well with the physiological features of happiness such as brain activity, blood pressure and immune system responses.

We can also look at the so-called happiness hormones to back up reported levels of happiness (Dfarhud et al. 2014). These include:

- Dopamine – a neurotransmitter (a chemical that transmits messages inside the brain) that is associated with high levels of positive mood. At least some of our happiness is thought to be caused by dopamine.

- Serotonin – another neurotransmitter which is associated with satisfaction, happiness and optimism.

- ⋏ Endorphins – activities such as walking, running, workouts, laughing, meditation and listening to music are all responsible for the release of endorphins, either directly or indirectly as they act as a stimulus to release this hormone. Endorphins give us strength, confidence and a mood of wellbeing and happiness.

- ⋏ Oxytocin – a hormone which facilitates our relationship with others and is associated with positive social behaviours. Good relationships have a strong effect on life satisfaction and there is a significant correlation between happiness and social relationship. So oxytocin can be a mechanism that produces happiness through facilitating social relations.

Perhaps in the future we will be able to measure happiness by monitoring the level of these hormones in the population. Until that happens, there is real value in simply asking people about their mood, as their answers tend to correlate with the levels of these hormones.

The next three sections will show data on how happy we are in the UK taken from the ONS based on survey data. They focus on the remaining Maslow levels of social, esteem and self-actualisation needs.

Social wellbeing

The importance of having friends and social connections for our personal wellbeing sounds intuitively right, so it's no surprise that it has a place on Maslow's hierarchy. In fact, social interaction has been proven to produce mental health benefits. This is brought to light in UK government research that was the springboard for a set of 'five-a-day' tips to help people maximise their mental wellbeing (see Chapter 8). Two out of the five tips related to social contact:

1. Connect with the people around you. With family, friends, colleagues and neighbours, at home, work, school or in your local community. Think of these as the cornerstones of your life and invest time in developing them. Building these connections will support and enrich you every day.

2. Do something nice for a friend or a stranger. Thank someone. Smile. Volunteer your time. Join a community group. Look out, as well as in. Seeing yourself and your happiness as linked to the wider community can be incredibly rewarding and creates connections with the people around you.

The question is, how can we measure social contact? Could it be measured by how many Facebook friends a person has? But what about people who don't use Facebook? And are 200 distant friends really as valuable as one or two close ones? How do you define 'friend'?

In his book *How Many Friends Does One Person Need?* (2010), Professor Robin Dunbar appears to have an answer. He describes a correlation between the size of the neocortex relative to the body size of different mammals and the size of the group that each of those mammals typically lives with. For example, baboons will typically live in a certain-sized social group, whereas lions will live in a different-sized group. By extrapolating these figures based on the size of the neocortex of humans, we can work out the ideal number of social connections a person should have. In this case, the answer was 150. This has become known as the Dunbar number.

Dunbar reported further research which substantiates that number. For example, he discovered that Iron Age tribes were typically around 150 people. But he also found a modern-day example that lends further weight to the Dunbar number theory: Gore-Tex factories. By trial and error, the waterproof clothing manufacturer has developed a business model that restricts each factory to 150 employees. If demand for the waterproof fabric is high and Gore-Tex needs to expand production, they will only increase existing factories until they have 150 people. After that, they prefer to open a new factory rather than keep expanding the same one. That's because they found that job satisfaction – and therefore production – was greater in factories where a maximum of 150 people worked.

The UK's Office of National Statistics (ONS) started to collect wellbeing data as early as 2011. One of the questions in the 2011 survey was, 'Please tell me how satisfied you are with your social life, using a scale from 1 to 10 where 1 means you are very dissatisfied with social life and 10 means you are very satisfied with social life.' Incidentally, the UK answers were compared to similar surveys around the rest of Europe. The average answer for the UK was 7.0 (ie 70 per cent); the highest in Europe was Denmark with an average of 8.3 and the lowest was Bulgaria with an average of 5.9.

Since that initial report there have been a couple of iterations on the type of data the ONS collects regularly. In 2017 the questions and answers were as follows:

- Those living with or married to a partner were asked to rate their happiness in their relationship on a scale from 'extremely unhappy' to 'perfect'. The middle point – 'happy' – represented the degree of happiness of most relationships. The percentage of people who were either 'very happy', 'extremely happy' or 'perfect' was 59.92 per cent. This was a decrease from the 2010 data where the equivalent figure was 67.20 per cent. The reports didn't reflect on the causes of this decrease, but the UK was recovering from the impacts of the credit crunch at the time, so perhaps that was a factor. The unhappiest were in Wales and the happiest were in Northern Ireland.

- Adults aged 16 and over across England were asked to state how often they felt lonely: often/always, some of the time, occasionally, hardly ever or never. 4.06 per cent of those surveyed answered 'often/always' compared to 4.92 per cent in 2014.

⋏ People were asked whether they had a spouse or partner, family member or friend they could rely on if they had a serious problem. In 2014, 84.04 per cent said they could rely on those people 'a lot'. This was a decrease from the 2011 figure of 86.08 per cent.

Between 3 April 2020 and 3 May 2020, during the Covid-19 lockdown, 5 per cent of people in Great Britain (2.6 million adults) reported that they felt lonely 'often' or 'always'. Surprisingly, this was about the same proportion as pre-lockdown. However, this is a slightly worse figure than back in 2014 and a later report showed an even worse picture: the figure for England was 7.26 per cent, Wales 8.25 per cent and Scotland 6.47 per cent (ONS 2021c).

It seems that external impacts – for example the credit crunch and the pandemic – really do have an effect on our social connection. It also appears that measuring social connection is possible and that results can be tracked and related to these outside factors. For the purposes of our matrix on page vii, we can use the latest figure for how satisfied we are with our social life, which was 7.0 out of 10.

I'm bloody brilliant, I am

According to Maslow, having high levels of esteem is also a human need. In fact, esteem is a need that must be satisfied in order for humans to achieve maximum wellbeing. Again, research from the Foresight Mental Capital and Wellbeing Project (2008) shows that low self-esteem can contribute to mental disorders. The report goes on to say that esteem is 'affected by a wide range of issues such as employment, housing, urbanisation, exposure to crime, and debt'.

Therefore, esteem is an essential need and again psychologists measure it by standard questionnaires. One measure is the Rosenberg Self-Esteem scale (RSE). The scale consists of 10 questions that respondents are asked to answer on a scale from 'strongly agree' to 'strongly disagree'. However, a 2001 study noted that one of the flaws with this approach was that people got fed up with answering multiple questions (Robins et al. 2001). The authors of the study wanted to see if the scale could be narrowed down to a single question: 'How much do you agree with the statement, "I have high self-esteem"?' Their results correlated well with the answers from the full RSE, showing once again that simply asking people how they rate their self-esteem gives a reasonably accurate measure.

The paper also included some insights about self-esteem. In one study researchers were interested in students who had taken an exam. The students were asked how well they thought they had performed in the exam before they knew the actual result. The same students were also assessed for their levels of self-esteem. The study found that the students with high levels of self-esteem reckoned that they would score highly on the exam, whereas students with low self-esteem didn't think they would score so highly. When the results came out, it was found that the average exam scores for both sets of students were the same. So although self-esteem is a necessary component of our human wellbeing, it isn't necessarily a good predictor of skill or competence.

The ONS also includes a related question in its wellbeing surveys. It asks respondents to rate out of 10 their answer to this: 'Overall, to what extent do you feel that the things you do in your life are worthwhile?' It then reports the percentage of people who reply with a very high rating. In London in 2013 this was 30.1 per cent, which, although positive, leads us to question why the remaining 69.9 per cent did not think they did worthwhile things.

Maslow's concept of esteem is helpfully defined by Di Domenico & Fournier (2017) as follows:

… a broad category of motivations that consist of two distinct but related sets of strivings. One set of esteem needs consists of people's desires for achievement, competence and mastery. The other set of esteem needs consists of people's desires for admiration, status and respect from others. Maslow (1943) described the satisfaction of esteem motives as being reflected in feelings of efficacy and confidence, and the thwarting of these desires in feelings of discouragement and inferiority.

So it seems that asking people about how worthwhile the things they do are fits very neatly with this definition. Although our average mark out of 10 (where 0 is 'not at all worthwhile' and 10 is 'completely worthwhile') has increased steadily from 7.6 in 2011 to just over 7.8 in 2021, this does mean that there is a general gap between current feelings and the ideal state where we'd all be marking ourselves 10 out of 10.

We can, however, use the 7.8 out of 10 directly in our average scoring matrix on page vii.

Self-actualisation

According to Maslow, self-actualisation is the pinnacle of what it means to be human. It is a state where a person has many 'peak experiences'. As explained in the introduction, this is not restricted to generally accepted views of what it is to be a high-performing individual. It is equally not an all-or-nothing state but represents the intensity and frequency of peak experiences, which for people with high self-actualisation will be much higher than for average people in current society. In his book *Toward a Psychology of Being* (1962), Maslow even refers to mystic and religious literature.

As we've discussed, Maslow says that an individual will only seek peak experiences after satisfying other needs. As for social and esteem needs, the key question is how to measure the degree of self-actualisation in individuals and in the population. One

69

approach might be to assume that any time left over after satisfying all other needs would give individuals enough time to pursue the things that help them self-actualise. Indeed, assessing the amount of free time individuals had was a method used by the same researchers who proved Maslow's theories correct (Tay & Diener 2011).

Back in 2013 the nearest relevant question from the ONS wellbeing data was the percentage who were 'completely satisfied with their amount of leisure time'. In 2013, this was a disappointing 13.6 per cent. In recent times the ONS tends not to report this or an equivalent figure. However, perhaps if people have reached self-actualisation, then their life satisfaction is complete and this is a figure that is regularly reported.

In response to the question 'Overall, how satisfied are you with your life nowadays?', the average answer in 2011 was 7.37 (ONS 2021d). It peaked at 7.72 in 2018 but by 2020, after Covid-19 hit, it had dropped again to 7.50. However, due to the pandemic the ONS only collected statistics by telephone, whereas before there were mixed modes of data collection, including face-to-face interviews. Wales, England and Scotland averaged 7.38 each, but Northern Ireland had an average of 7.54.

For our matrix on page vii we can use the satisfaction with leisure time answer of 13.6 per cent to calculate our wellbeing for self-actualisation. To convert this to marks out of 5 we can simply multiply the figure by 0.05, which gives 0.7 out of 5. So you can see that we are not reaching our full happiness potential. Our esteem is below what it could be and our self-actualisation – the highest level on Maslow's scale – is a mere 0.7 out of 5. In the chapters that follow we will see that not only can we increase these scores by making small changes to our behaviour but these changes can have an impact on the lower Maslow levels, too. Is it really too good to be true that there could be a formula for happiness on both a basic and a metaphysical level? Let's see.

Chapter 5
Our homes

In Chapter 3 I looked at the current state of our physical wellbeing in terms of our environmental impacts and how they interact with the security of supply of our basic needs such as air quality, food security, water supply and protection of our shelter. I observed that, despite having most of our basic needs met in the UK, we are nevertheless at risk of floods, overheating, food insecurity and other crises. This is largely due to our own environmental impacts.

So what can we do about it? In this chapter I'll look at how the sustainability of our homes, the ways we get out and about and what we buy have an impact on the planet as well as our own happiness. Then we will see what actions we can take to decrease our environmental impacts and, in turn, help contribute to our long-term wellbeing.

Roughly a third of the UK's carbon emissions come from our homes. This is either directly through burning gas in our boilers or indirectly by using electricity which comes from power stations that burn fossil fuels. This means that the more we can do to reduce the energy use of our homes, the less carbon we'll emit. Done right, it also means a warmer, cosier home and cheaper bills.

We can split the emissions from our homes into what are termed regulated and unregulated emissions in the UK. Regulated emissions are those that arise chiefly from the fabric of the home (ie levels of insulation) and the heating system. Unregulated emissions generally arise from electrical appliances that we plug in, such as fridges and TVs.

Dealing with regulated emissions is generally within the realm of the homeowner. So owner-occupiers have a huge influence on what gets done. For renters, it's generally the landlord who will have the greatest influence. In this section I'll look at what's needed regardless of tenure, but for renters there is a section on how to convince your landlord to make improvements.

Regulated emissions

Roughly three quarters of the emissions from the average home come from space heating and water heating. This will vary considerably between homes but generally speaking this average holds true. Reducing regulated emissions is a fast-moving field in the UK. New technologies and new methodologies for establishing best practice are rapidly changing. Nevertheless there are some consistent rules of thumb that can be followed to ensure your home is at a sustainable level of energy efficiency.

The first thing to know is how domestic energy efficiency calculations work. The formal way of doing this is through the standard assessment procedure or SAP. SAP looks at:

- fabric efficiency – the insulation levels of your roof, floor, walls, windows and doors
- heating system – type and efficiency
- lighting efficiency
- use of pumps and fans – used to circulate heat around the home
- size and efficiency of solar photovoltaic (PV) panels
- cooling, eg air conditioning.

A calculation is then made to estimate how much gas, electricity or other fuel the people in the home buy. Taking the above conditions into account, this is converted into a SAP rating from 0 to 100. The higher the SAP rating, the less fuel the homeowner buys. A rating of 100 would mean the homeowner isn't buying any fuel at all. This is possible but quite rare.

The SAP rating also relates to the perhaps more familiar energy performance certificate or EPC. Since 2008, whenever you buy or rent a home the seller or landlord must show you this certificate. It rates the home on a scale from A to G, A being a very energy-efficient home that will not cost much to keep warm and G being an energy-inefficient home that will cost a lot to keep warm. Here's how the SAP ratings relate to the EPC rating along with some other details to give you an idea of what the ratings mean:

SAP rating	EPC band	Comment
92+	A	This would be an ideal new build standard.
81–91	B	Most new build homes in 2021 were EPC B. In my consultancy work, we estimate that the average SAP for homes in the UK should be 85 by 2050 to reflect net zero status.
69–80	C	Achieving EPC C for existing homes is in most government strategies.
55–68	D	The average SAP rating in England is 65.
39–54	E	The absolute minimum energy efficiency that private renters are allowed. From 2025 newly rented properties will be required to be at band C; likewise by 2028 for existing rentals.
21–38	F	Illegal for private renters to let out (with some exemptions).
1–20	G	Illegal for private renters to let out (with some exemptions).

You will note that the SAP rating is based on the cost of heating and not on carbon emissions. Some people criticise the methodology because of this but the reality is that, if you are not buying fuel, you are not emitting any carbon. So low cost will always be low carbon and the data in the UK bears that out. However, the reverse is not always true. Not all low-carbon homes are cheap to run. An example of this is wood pellet boilers. Wood pellets are low carbon, as the wood grown to make the pellets absorbs the same amount of carbon that is emitted when the wood pellets are burned. There is of course extra carbon emitted due to processing and transport but they are still very low carbon compared to other fuel sources. However, they are expensive to buy, so a low carbon home that uses wood pellets will not be cheap to run.

Another criticism of SAP is the quality of the assessments. The regulatory requirement is a) the SAP assessor is qualified and quality monitored; b) they visit the home to make their assessment; and c) they lodge the results using a recognised body, which then produces the EPC certificate. However, the reality is that home visits are not always accurate. For example, the assessor might list a home as having double glazing throughout when actually it has single glazing.

If your home has had an EPC done you can download it from this website: find-energy-certificate.digital.communities.gov.uk As well as telling you what rating you have, the certificate will also give you a list of recommendations to make improvements, a rough idea of the cost and an idea of what it will do to your SAP rating.

So what SAP rating should you aim for? There is no national policy on what SAP rating represents net zero but there is an emerging pathway that gives a good steer (Committee on Climate Change 2020).

1. Improve energy efficiency so that each home is EPC C.

2. Switch to electric heating systems.

3. Achieve net zero for the national electricity grid.

From this pathway, our consultancy has calculated that the average SAP rating for the UK should be SAP 85 by 2050. Let's expand on these issues.

Improving energy efficiency so that each home is EPC C

Ideally this will be achieved through fabric measures, eg insulating roofs, walls, windows, doors and in some cases floors. Insulation means homes have low energy demand and fabric measures are often the most cost effective to make, albeit not the most exciting. Most government policies – for example, those on fuel poverty – target EPC level C, and this is also the level required by investors. The Committee on Climate Change recommends that investors' mortgage portfolios only apply to homes with EPC C or better. This may mean that selling a house that is less than EPC C may be more difficult in the future.

For some homes this level might be hard to achieve. There might be planning issues due to heritage status that affect the ability to insulate the outside of homes or upgrade windows to double glazing, for example. There are still options for these homes but they tend to involve internal wall insulation, which is disruptive and may be better suited to installation when the whole home gets upgraded.

Another way to upgrade the home is by using solar PV panels that use the sun's energy to generate electricity. If you have a roof facing the right way, these are a viable way of getting to EPC C and future-proofing the home. However, the current SAP methodology 'over-rewards' solar PV, so future versions of SAP may not give as many points for panels. Nevertheless, they will be rewarded and will help with future heating systems. Target dates to achieve EPC C vary from 2028 to 2035 depending on the tenure of the property and whose roadmap to net zero you want to follow.

Switching to electric heating systems

For domestic properties the general direction of travel is to switch to electric heating systems. That said, there are other low-carbon heating technologies, one of which might become available for your home. However, for planning purposes it would be prudent to assume that most houses will switch to electric heating for now.

The most likely solution for widespread electric heating is the use of heat pumps. Heat pumps are an established technology that capture heat from either the surrounding air, the ground, water sources or even exhaust warm air from other homes. The key benefit is that for every unit of energy you pay to power the pump, you get more energy in the form of heat. So, air source heat pumps may give you 3 kWh of heat for every kWh of electricity you buy and ground source heat pumps might give you 4 or more kWh of heat for every kWh of electricity you buy. This increase in energy gained is called the coefficient of performance (COP). If you get 3 kWh of heat from 1 kWh of electricity, you will have a COP of 3.

Improvements in our electricity grid recently mean that for every kWh of electricity used about 0.25 kg of CO_2 is emitted. For every kWh of gas used, the equivalent carbon emissions are about 0.2 kg. Incidentally, this is a lot less than your EPC will tell you. As described above, the SAP methodology is not perfect and one of the measurements that needs updating is the CO_2 emissions for electricity. SAP still uses a figure of around 0.5 kg CO_2 per kWh of electricity, which is twice the actual rate from the grid.

So you can see that heat pumps only need to achieve a COP of 1.25 or more to emit less CO_2 for the same amount of heat generated. Pretty much all heat pumps achieve a higher COP than this. The key issue at the moment is that electricity in the UK costs a lot more than gas. This means that replacing an old gas boiler with a heat pump may result in higher running costs than if you simply replaced the old boiler with a new more efficient boiler.

There are moves in government to change the prices of domestic gas and electricity by changing various taxes or levies that are built into the pricing. If this is successful it will most likely pave the way for people to swap their gas boilers for heat pumps. In any case, the emerging pathways to net zero suggest that the last boiler replacement should be around 2033, so there is plenty of time.

Having said all of this, there are some homes that are ideal for switching to a heat pump now. Well-insulated homes that are not on mains gas are prime candidates. These are homes that currently run off LPG, oil or electric storage heaters. The home must be well insulated, however. (See below for more on heat pumps.)

Net zero grid

In the past ten years the way we generate electricity in the UK has changed dramatically – and for the better. We've almost got rid of coal-fired power stations and increased the amount of wind and solar capacity. All this has led to a huge reduction in what is called carbon intensity, ie the amount of CO_2 emitted per kWh of electricity used. And this decrease is set to continue up to 2050 at least. This will be achieved through more renewable capacity, probably (and sadly in my view) a bit of nuclear and buying power from hydroelectricity from other countries such as Norway. There will most likely also be some kind of storage capacity so we can capture energy when the sun shines or the wind blows but we don't need to use that energy straight away.

If there are any fossil fuel-burning power stations left by then, the plan is either to sequester any emitted CO_2, for example by pumping it into sealed holes in the ground, or the CO_2 will be 'offset' by planting enough forest to absorb that same amount of carbon. So, in one way or another, by 2050 the electricity grid will be at net zero. However, no matter what is done about how it is generated, there is still a massive need to reduce the demand for power in our homes. This is because there will be other sectors competing for electricity, most notably transport and electric vehicles.

If you don't like that plan and you fancy a go at doing better, you might enjoy the online game Climate 2050 at 2050-calcula-tor-tool.decc.gov.uk (see also mackaycarboncalculator.beis.gov.uk). Your goal is to reduce CO_2 emissions for the UK by 80 per cent (this was the old target based on 1990 levels of emissions). To set a benchmark, I managed to achieve the reduction target without resorting to nuclear, which I don't think is a sustainable solution. However, this book is about reducing environmental impacts at household and organisation level, not about national policies. So, on a personal basis, what technologies should you use?

What technology should I use?

Deciding which is the best solution for your own home can be difficult. The best pros and cons approach I've seen is at simple energyadvice.org.uk/pages/green-homes-grant. It was developed in conjunction with a government department so there are no commercial interests behind it (the grant itself is no longer available). However, if you want to make a start thinking about how you could upgrade your home, below is a list of the various interventions you can make together with some pros and cons of each. Bear in mind that this is an overview and the nature of each product will vary between suppliers and installers and what's suitable for your home. It should go without saying that you should check the credentials of any company undertaking work on your property and that all work should have guarantees. You may want to include these upgrades when you are doing other things to your home such as an extension, heating system upgrade, roof replacement or loft conversion. These are all good opportunities to make improvements while the relevant tradespeople are on site.

Cavity wall insulation

This is a very good and easy improvement that is suitable for most homes. The only exceptions would be homes exposed to driving rain, at high risk of flooding or with thin cavities. Installers 'blow' insulating beads into the cavity and the home is warmer as a result. Modern homes will most likely have their cavities already filled, while older homes may have been filled with glass or mineral fibre wool. In some cases these might have sagged over time. One indicator of this is if there are cold spots towards the top part of your walls or even mould growth in these areas. In these cases it may be necessary to extract older insulation and replace it with beads.

Loft insulation

This is easy and cheap and, in most cases, can be done yourself. Aim for a minimum of 300 mm – there's only minor benefit beyond that thickness. Because most joists are only 150 mm thick, if you want to board over the insulation, you will also need to buy and install stilts that raise the boards above the insulation. And of course, the job might be made harder if you have a lot of stuff in your loft, but then again, it may be a chance for a clear-out.

External wall insulation (EWI)

EWI is trickier to install and more costly than cavity wall insulation but it is one of two options if the walls of your home are solid (this should be indicated on the EPC certificate). Installation also creates more disruption because installers have to remove drainpipes and other items attached to the external wall before the insulation can go on. However, once it's done it will make a huge difference to your comfort and bills. The other benefit is that it makes the home look a lot nicer, which is particularly good if you don't like the external appearance of your home.

Generally, you don't need planning permission for EWI but for some homes, planning may be an issue in your area. Heritage homes and homes in conservation areas may be affected, for example, although the application of conservation rules seems to vary hugely throughout the UK, so you may be able to argue your case. One option is to apply brick 'slips' to the EWI, which will still make it look like the rest of the conservation area.

If you are not ready to install EWI but can envision doing it at some time in the future then there are a couple of things worth thinking about when undertaking other works in your home. For example, if you are having the roof replaced, consider extending the eaves of the roof to cover over the top of any future EWI. Similarly if you are having a replacement boiler, make sure the flue is extended ready for future EWI. Of course, this might not be so relevant as we move to electric heating systems.

Internal wall insulation

This is the other option for solid walls. It is a disruptive process because it has implications for skirting boards and coving, etc, and it also reduces room sizes a little bit. Internal wall insulation is best installed when you are gutting a home or when the home is otherwise empty. Preventing condensation is also important, so proper installers are critical for this work. The cost is similar to EWI. There is also a small downside when it comes to overheating risk (see the overheating section). When the sun hits the outer wall of a house, the wall absorbs the heat and re-radiates it later in the day. Internal wall insulation reduces the wall's ability to cool down. However, if you have other overheating risk measures in place then this risk can be countered.

Floor insulation

This sometimes comes up as a recommendation on EPCs. As with internal wall insulation, installing floor insulation is best done when the downstairs rooms are empty. Options include laying insulation on top of a solid floor where there is sufficient ceiling height or, if you have wooden floors, insulation can be installed under the floor in special nets. For suspended wooden floors small robots can be used to crawl underneath the floor and install foam insulation.

Windows and doors

If you haven't got them already, double- or triple-glazed windows will add a couple of SAP points to your home. Other benefits of modern windows include no drafts and reduced outside noise. Look for the lowest 'U' value when choosing between different suppliers and make sure they have trickle vents in case ventilation is a problem after installation.

Gas boilers

At the time of writing mains gas is cheaper than other sources of domestic energy (except self-generated electricity). Upgrading your boiler, especially if it is old, will make a huge difference. Although the future of heating will be electric, the chances are that at the moment replacing your gas boiler with a modern one will result in lower bills than, say, replacing your old boiler with an air source heat pump. The current plan is for the last gas boiler replacement to happen roughly in the year 2033 (they won't be allowed in new homes from 2025). In other words, if you have a G-rated gas boiler, you could replace with a new A-rated one and wait till next time to upgrade to a heat pump. Or you could go straight for a heat pump (see next section) and be ready for the future but your bills will be higher in the short term compared to an A-rated gas boiler. That said, there are many promotions, grants and payment schemes that may balance that out.

But is it the case that it's always better for the planet to replace your boiler? What about the waste of scrapping an old but functioning boiler in order to install a more efficient one? Here's what the situation was in our house:

- ▲ The boiler was old but working fine.
- ▲ The efficiency was 68 per cent.
- ▲ The latest service report indicated that future repairs would be difficult due to parts availability.
- ▲ We wanted to move the boiler out of the kitchen where it was taking up cupboard space.
- ▲ We needed to drain the system anyway to install TRV radiator controls.
- ▲ The commercial sector is under its own pressure to recycle more, so I wasn't too bothered about scrapping the old boiler.
- ▲ The new boiler would be 98 per cent efficient.

The combination of those factors led me to choose a new A-rated boiler. Next time the boiler needs replacing I will choose a heat pump. What about combi boilers versus hot water storage? Theoretically, combi boilers are cheaper to run but in practice this is disputable, so if you already have hot water storage it's inadvisable to swap it for a combi boiler. Also, the heating systems of the future will be more efficient if hot water storage is available.

Heat pumps

These work by extracting heat out of the surrounding area. The most common types are air source (which extract heat out of surrounding air) and ground source (which extract heat from the ground). Other types, albeit less common, include water source, which normally extract heat from rivers, and exhaust air, which normally work with mechanically ventilated homes. A heat pump is likely to save you money and CO_2 emissions compared to your existing system if your home is well insulated and is currently off gas, ie is heated using LPG, coal, oil or electricity.

But how do heat pumps work? How can it be possible to extract more kWh of heat than the kWh of electricity you buy? Remember that, even on a cold day, there is always some heat in the air: even if it is -5°C outside the heat pump can extract something. In fact, heat pumps are an established technology – the same technology has long been used, albeit in reverse, for keeping our fridges cool and for air conditioning. So it's not some kind of black magic.

As we saw earlier in the chapter, the equivalent of efficiency for heat pumps is coefficient of performance (COP). The higher the COP, the more heat it extracts from the surrounding area. The ground is typically higher in temperature throughout the year than the air, so ground pumps typically have better COP than air pumps. However, the downside is that ground source heat pumps are more complex to install, as a long pipe must be inserted into the ground – either horizontally in a very long ditch or vertically in a deep borehole (local geology permitting). Air source heat pumps, on the other hand, are simply mounted on the outside of the wall.

The system also requires radiators or underfloor heating, and even if you already have radiators they may need to be replaced with slightly bigger ones. This is because the temperature in the heating system will be lower than a gas boiler system, so you have to run it for longer to get the same amount of heat into each room. One last point to remember on heat pumps is to ensure you get a good quality one and that there is maintenance and repair capacity in your area.

Hydrogen

There is currently a lot of news about hydrogen boilers. Unlike natural gas or methane, burning hydrogen in suitable boilers does not produce CO_2 emissions and, as hydrogen boilers can be swapped like for like with gas ones, people with gas boilers have an easy switch when they need to replace their existing system. The downsides are as follows:

- The vast majority of hydrogen is currently produced from methane, so CO_2 is generated at the production sites.

- Although hydrogen can be generated using renewables, there are associated inefficiencies and it may be better to use renewable electricity directly.

- The hydrogen molecule is smaller than the methane molecule and so can escape out of smaller holes in our gas mains network. This means the network will need upgrading.

- Although burning hydrogen in air does not produce CO_2 emissions, it does produce nitrogen oxides, which are a local air pollutant.

At the moment the list of downsides looks far longer than the upsides and yet hydrogen boilers still keep appearing in government strategies. Until the potential disadvantages are ironed out, it would be wiser to plan for a switch to electric. Then, if by some luck you end up near a renewable and cheap source of hydrogen in the future, you can still upgrade your heating system to hydrogen. Either way, there will most likely be a huge market for hydrogen in the future but this will probably be reserved for things like steel works and heavy-duty machinery, not domestic heating.

Other electric

Storage heaters, panel heaters and infrared heaters all have a place in heating homes, especially if other heating options aren't suitable (eg there is no space for a heat pump). They are less efficient than heat pumps but very easy to install. It's worth noting that infrared heaters aren't currently recognised in SAP at the moment other than as an electric heater. However, the makers claim that they are more efficient because they only heat the surfaces that the infrared rays hit and not the air in between. This means that if that air escapes through holes in the fabric of the house or through ventilation, there is no heat lost. This means they should be more efficient than storage or panel heaters. However, this claim is not recognised yet in SAP. As with anything, quality is key with these systems, and older storage heaters are definitely worth replacing.

Mechanical ventilation with heat recovery (MVHR)

It is unlikely that MVHR will be a retrofit option for an existing home unless it is being completely gutted but it is being fitted in new homes. The principle is that the warm air from warm rooms (eg the kitchen and bathroom) is extracted via a ducting system, passed through a heat exchanger and the heat transferred to new, fresh incoming air that is pumped into bedrooms and living rooms. These systems are useful for well-insulated homes where ventilation is critical. Such homes typically have no leaky fabric like older homes, so an actual fan and ducting system are needed to pump stale air out of the home. The stale air comes from condensation and CO_2 from exhaling, smells from cooking and other pollutants like chemicals from carpets or odours from pets.

These homes typically need very little extra heat input because so much heat from solar gains, human activity and cooking is already recycled via the MVHR system. They are one of the key principles for the low-energy Passivhaus standard. The electricity needed to run the circulating fan is minimal. It also means that you can get excellent ventilation, filtered incoming air and, because you can keep the windows closed while ventilating, reduced external noise coming into your home.

MVHR is an established system, particularly in colder countries, but it is not so ubiquitous in the UK. If I were to build my own home, I would definitely use MVHR for all the reasons given above. As ever, quality is everything and there are various reports of things going wrong with MVHR due to poor installation. Here are some things to watch out for:

- Noise from the fan – either the fan has not been enclosed in the right soundproofing or the ducting has not been installed correctly. For example, the wrong material or bent ducting pipes can cause noisy air circulation.

- Air filter installed in an inaccessible place – unbelievably, this has been reported. The filter must be washed or replaced a couple of times a year and also soon after occupying a new home (to get rid of building dust in the air). For this reason it needs to be somewhere you can get hold of it regularly and ideally with sensors to let you know when to replace it.

There is no formal accreditation for MVHR installers, so care must be taken to identify good quality installers.

For ultra eco-warriors – and if you can find the right techie guys to do it – there is also a system of passive stack ventilation with heat recovery. This is where there is no fan to pump air around the ducting system but the circulation is achieved by exploiting different air pressures between ground level and the top of the stack or long vertical pipe. It is tricky to pull off but if installed successfully is a low-maintenance system with no moving parts.

Wood burners

Logs or pellets still emit CO_2 when burned but that CO_2 is theoretically reabsorbed when replacement wood is grown, so wood burning is a relatively low-carbon option. There is a small amount of embodied carbon because of processing and transport but by and large most of the CO_2 emitted is reabsorbed. The main issue with wood burners is the other pollutants that come from burning wood, mainly nitrogen oxides and particulate matter (PMs). Depending on what system you have there's also maintenance, cleaning, fuel cost and fuel storage to consider. For this reason wood burners are likely not the answer on a large scale but some people like the appeal. If you get a wood burner, care must be taken to ensure that it is allowed in your area and Defra approved.

Heating controls

The best advice on heating controls is to install as many as you can and learn how to use them. After some cold days and a bit of experimenting you'll get used to the way your home heats up and cools down and you get a good feel of how the timers and radiator controls can be set. They cost a little more but you can also buy heating controls that quickly 'learn' how you and your home behaves and set timings and controls for you. The manufacturers of these devices report typical 15 per cent savings.

One key thing is that using the thermostat as an on/off switch is the least efficient way of running your heating system. This will be even more relevant when we switch to electric heating systems, except for the infrared panels.

We will never resolve the argument of different people feeling different temperatures in the same household but we are probably all familiar with one family member wearing multiple jumpers and still claiming it's freezing while another walks round in shorts and T-shirt. Suffice to say that heating calculations are based on the home being 21°C during the heating period on the assumption that is the average desired temperature and aligns with World Health Organization thermal comfort levels. It is also worth noting that turning down the heating system to 21°C from a higher temperature will save money and CO_2 emissions.

Solar PV

If you can afford solar panels, it is wise to place as many as you can on your roof. The various grants for installing them have gone but you can still get paid for exporting electricity to the grid. Of course, you'll get the biggest saving from generating electricity to power your new electric heating system. Combined with battery storage (which is still pricey at the time of writing), solar panels potentially offer massive savings. There are even some people who are getting paid by the power companies while they have free heating. When installing solar panels you'll need to consider shading from trees, other buildings and chimneys. Also remember that the inverters used to transform the generated electricity into AC for the home will need replacing and the quoted timescale is every 15 years.

If you are replacing a roof, some manufacturers claim that they can install solar PV tiles cheaper than traditional materials. Integrated solar PV, ie those that form part or all of the roof, look better. One downside of surface-mounted panels is that birds like to nest underneath them. Depending on your viewpoint, you may or may not like this but if it's undesirable then a little bit of netting around the side should deal with that.

Solar PV is currently over-rewarded on the SAP system, so it can't be relied on to get your home to EPC C. Batteries aren't rewarded yet but they most likely will be in the next version.

Solar thermal

These are panels that sit on your roof and heat up water one way or another. You'll probably see that they don't add many SAP points to your EPC rating and they will also compete for roof space with any solar PV. Although they provide free hot water, personally I would generate as much electricity from my roof as I can. Electricity is more flexible, surplus can be used elsewhere and there are no moving parts or pumps. I find it's also easier to check that the solar PV system is working.

Wind turbines

The latest reports indicate that wind turbines don't work that well in a typical domestic property, although they sometimes appear as a recommendation in windy areas.

Lighting

Lights are also part of regulated emissions and energy efficient ones (ie LED) tend to add a SAP point to your rating. LEDs are much better than the older compact fluorescent lamps (CFLs) that flooded the market a decade or so ago and took forever to get bright. These gave energy-efficient lighting a bad name, but things have come on a lot since then and LEDs are worth the investment.

Marks out of tenancy

Of course, many people don't own their own homes, so it's important to consider those people who are in rented accommodation or who otherwise don't have the full control of their homes to make energy efficiency improvements. There are certainly things you can do about unregulated emissions (appliances you plug in – see below) and you can learn how to use your heating controls. But dealing with the fabric of the home and any new heating systems will be more challenging.

Due to the lack of suitable accommodation in the UK it's also not so easy to vote with your feet. You have the option to speak with your landlord and point out that the forthcoming plan is to get to EPC C (if your home isn't at that rating already). In the private rented sector (notoriously the worst-performing sector in the UK in terms of energy) landlords are regulated via the minimum energy efficiency standard (MEES). Under this scheme it is currently illegal for private sector landlords to rent out anything EPC G or F (with a few exceptions), but by 2030 the minimum threshold will be EPC C, so it is in your landlord's best interests to aim to attain this level. EPC C may also become a mortgage lender requirement, so this is another approach you can take with your landlord. MEES is regulated via your local authority, so if talks with your landlord haven't worked and you feel comfortable about taking the issue further, then you can get help at council level.

For social housing tenants, there is no equivalent regulation in England, although Wales and Scotland do have a minimum SAP rating. However, the Social Housing White Paper (DLUHC 2020) strongly hints that EPC C will soon be a regulatory requirement and the sector is certainly gearing up for that.

If all that fails there is a great initiative called Marks out of Tenancy (marksoutoftenancy.com). It works like Tripadvisor but for rented accommodation. When people leave an accommodation, they can rate it about anything, including energy efficiency and how well (or not) the landlord dealt with other environmental issues. Granted, this won't directly benefit you but the next person looking at the property will be forewarned and you can check Marks out of Tenancy before you take on a new rental. Perhaps it will also spur more private sector landlords to improve the environmental performance of rented accommodation.

Unregulated emissions

So far, I've talked about regulated emissions, which are largely about the fabric of the home and the heating system. These all feed into the calculations for a home's SAP and EPC ratings. However, there are many aspects of the home that don't get included in the SAP calculations but, if you improve their efficiency, will still save you money and reduce CO_2 emissions.

There are many excellent sources of information for improving unregulated emissions, including the Energy Saving Trust (energysavingtrust.org.uk), which was spun from a government initiative and has a good reputation. That said, here are some other tips for reducing unregulated emissions:

1. Turn lights off in unoccupied rooms (why is this so difficult for some people?).

2. If you are changing your kitchen, consider an induction hob. They use less electricity to heat food and are also easy to clean. They create less water vapour in the kitchen compared to burning gas and they are much more controllable than the old electric element-style cookers.

3. Get an energy monitor that gives you instant feedback on the amount of electricity you use. These are different from smart meters which, although useful, don't give instant feedback. Once installed you can run around the house turning things on or off and seeing how much electricity each appliance uses. I found a printer switched on and using electricity (in the transformer) and yet I rarely used it. A friend was shocked at how much electricity was used by leaving the fridge door open too long. This wasn't while the door was open but when the door was shut again the compressor had to work overtime to cool the fridge compartment.

4. Speaking of printers, if you are ready for it then consider getting rid of yours altogether. So many documents such as travel passes, fuel bills and holiday bookings are now done electronically that there is less need to print anything these days. Even documents you need to sign can be done electronically (see the SHIFT guide at shiftenvironment.co.uk/news/save-time-paper-and-ink-sign-pdf-forms-electronically). On the increasingly rare occasion that you do need to print something out, you can still do this at a local stationers or library. You will have to pay but there is no hassle with ink and getting the printer to work.

5. Only fill the kettle as much as you need it. I met a woman who would boil a whole kettle and let it cool down each day because she didn't trust the local water company.

6. Using electricity to heat anything is costly, so do what you can to reduce using anything hot. This may be a bonus for people who don't like ironing!

7. Buy white goods (fridges, dishwashers and washing machines) with the highest energy rating you can afford. The rating system is A–G, as per our homes, with A being the most efficient and G the least.

8. My auntie lives in an electrically heated house, complete with an immersion heater. However, she found that between the electric white goods and the electric shower, she rarely needed hot water from the cylinder and so she switched it off.

9. If you can, turn appliances off standby, particularly anything with a black transformer (printers, laptops). This is because transformers keep on working unless you switch them off at the wall. The same applies to electric toothbrushes.

10. Save hot water on showers. There is an overlap here with the saving water section later but because showers use hot water

it'll save energy too, so I'll include it here. Go to your water supplier's website and look for free water-saving devices. Among the offerings you'll find an aerating shower head or fitting. These devices fill the water droplets from the shower with air and make them, for want of a better term, fluffy. To your skin, where the touch receptors are far enough apart, the shower feels like a normal shower experience. And there's plenty to wash away soap, etc. They are easy to install and can reduce the flow rate from 11 litres/minute to 6 l/min. And remember that this is hot water, so that saves lots of heating bills. They also reduce the amount of steam in the bathroom, which is a bonus because this in turn reduces the chances of mould growth on tile grouting. They can even make the shower easier to clean. Aerated shower heads are most useful if you have a shower fed from the boiler and the flow rate is above 8 l/min (you can easily test with a jug and a stopwatch).

11. Save hot water on basin taps. As with showers you can order free aerating water tap fittings. These are best for wash basin taps, as kitchen taps are mostly used for filling kettles and saucepans so reduced flow would only make things longer to fill.

12. Save water in the bath. If you are replacing the bath look for a lower volume bath but make sure you are comfortable in it. You can also buy inflatable toys for children that stick to the bottom of the bath, thereby displacing some of the hot water, so you need less warm water to fill the bath to a decent depth.

13. Replace petrol tools such as lawnmowers, strimmers and hedge trimmers with electrical or rechargeable ones. These emit less CO_2 than the petrol alternatives.

Water usage

As you know, water is crucial and at the moment we are not using it in a sustainable manner. The ideal is about 130 litres per person per day (lpd), which is still plenty and a target that is well within reach with no discernible impact on our lives (see also Chapter 3).

The first step is to see how much water you are using. If you have a water meter, this is a simple step: just look at your usage in litres and divide this by the number of people in your home (your bill may show cubic metres – 1 m^3 is 1000 litres). Otherwise, your bill will normally say how many litres per day your household is using, so just divide by the number of people in your household. If the figure is less than 130 litres per person per day, then great – just keep an eye on it so it doesn't get out of hand. It's also good to monitor it because if it goes up all of a sudden it could indicate a leak.

If you don't have a water meter, consider getting one. Homes with meters typically use 10 lpd less than homes without meters. And bills normally go down compared to the old rates system. In any case, there may be a compulsory water meter installed in your area due to water stress.

If you don't want a meter but would still like to know your usage you can estimate it. This is especially fun if you like wading through calculations – the calculations used for UK building regulations are quite in depth – there's a calculator at wrcpartgcalculator.co.uk/Calculator.aspx. You will need to know things like the water capacity of your toilet cistern and the flow rates of taps – all calculations that you should be able to find. Then you multiply those values by the typical usage pattern. There are even average values for how often we go to the toilet and how often we turn taps on. When you have your final answer, don't forget to add on 10 lpd for your lack of water meter and this should give you an idea.

Here are some things you can do to reduce water usage. Some

of them are best implemented when you upgrade your bathroom but many of them you can do now:

1. If you have a large toilet cistern (more than 9 litres), you can get a water displacement device from your water company for free. This is simply a bag that fills with 1 litre of water and sits in your cistern. It keeps that 1 litre per flush behind, thereby saving with each flush. Plus, because it's an open-topped bag, the water gets refreshed so there is no chance of stale water building up.

2. Use showers more than baths, particularly if you have already installed the aerated shower head.

3. Get a free shower timer. This is a little egg timer that essentially turns having a shower into a game. Can you have a shower in four minutes?

4. This is an obvious one but just in case it hasn't reached you yet, turn off the tap when brushing your teeth. There really is no need to keep it running all the time.

5. Fit aerated tap fittings in cold wash basin taps. As before, you can get these for free from your water company.

6. If you have a garden and a drainpipe, you have all you need to install a rainwater butt. You can use this for watering your garden. You can get some imaginatively designed water butts these days, so it may well enhance the appearance of your garden, too.

7. Harvest rainwater. This is not an easy win and you can achieve 130 lpd without it by being clever with the other water devices in your home. But if you really must have high-flow showers and taps and a high-volume bath, then you can 'offset' your high water usage by harvesting rainwater. It requires professional installers, digging a big hole for your storage tank and then using a pump to pump the water to where you need it.

8. Grey water recycling is an approach that captures waste water from baths and wash basins and uses it for flushing toilets. There are various designs, from a simple sink attached to the top of the toilet cistern to rather complex bits of kit that filter and segregate the grey water before using it to flush. Again, there is no real need if you've achieved 130 lpd using efficient fittings elsewhere.

9. Use a compost toilet. I'm a chartered environmentalist and even I'm not ready for these yet. But if you're so inclined and have the right space for it, then why not? There are no moving parts so very little can go wrong and it does resolve disputes about leaving toilet lids up or down. They are down for everyone.

Making changes in the home is the single biggest effect you can have not only on your environmental impacts but also on your own happiness. Because as we've seen, our happiness at a basic and non-basic level is inextricably linked with our behaviours towards the environment around us. Most importantly, many of the changes we've discussed in this chapter are cheap to implement and do not have an adverse effect on your day-to-day life. And yet they reduce our risk of many events that threaten our wellbeing. On page 142, I'll look at how to rate these changes in the home to add to the happiness matrix.

Chapter 6
Improving security

Aside from our basic needs, one of the greatest threats to our happiness and overall wellbeing on the Maslow scale is the risk to our environmental and physical security. So how can we take reasonable steps to improve our wellbeing when it comes to flood, fire and famine? And what can we do to mitigate against threats to our homes and welfare in the form of crime?

Flood risk

Speaking to people whose homes have flooded reminds us that it truly is an awful experience. Not only is there the mess, damage and smell during the flood but there are often months of clean-up and drying out after the event. Anything you can do to prevent or prepare for flooding will help to avoid months of disruption.

You can easily check the flood risk of your property on the Environment Agency's flood risk map (gov.uk/check-long-term-flood-risk – be sure to use this one and not the one for planning). They update it regularly with the latest projections and modelling so it's best to check each year, say when renewing your buildings and contents insurance. Be sure to check all forms of flood risk, especially fluvial (river banks bursting) and surface water flooding (caused by too many impervious surfaces being installed, eg block paving). If you are in anything other than a low or very low flood risk zone, there are things you can do to prepare:

- ⌃ Sign up for the Environment Agency's flood alerts – this will give you a warning if a flood is expected in your area imminently.

- ⌃ Keep drains on your property clear and also keep an eye on the drains in your street. When my daughter was young, we had a lovely time picking big leaves from blocked drains and then watching the flood water on the road disappear with a whirl.

- ⌃ Think twice about paving over any areas on your property. I used to live in Germany and as well as your water charges the council levied a charge proportional to the amount of hard surface you had on the property. This is because the water companies have to deal with the run-off water. The charge prompted many people to install permeable surfaces. This doesn't have to mean gravel or grass. You can even get permeable block paved drives.

- ⌃ If your home is at risk of flooding, install flood barriers that slot into special guides for times when a flood is imminent. Seek professional help with these as there is a maximum height of around 0.9 m to prevent too much water building up on one side of the barrier. This could create too much pressure, and if the barrier is on the front door and the flood water is on your wall, this could cause structural damage or even collapse.

- ⌃ Check air bricks that may let in water and have a plan in place to block them during a flood alert. However, don't block them permanently because they are there for ventilation.

There are other things you can do to prevent the worst, many of which are covered in a guide I wrote some time ago called 'Your social housing in a changing climate' (London Climate Change

Partnership 2013). It may be that the best thing to do is let your home flood and enable a quick clean-up after the event. In this case, there are things you can do to minimise damage:

- ⚴ Consider installing downstairs kitchen units on waterproof plinths so at least the wood doesn't get damaged.

- ⚴ Ensure electrical wiring is above any predicted flood depth. This includes the main fuse box as well as electrical plug sockets.

- ⚴ Don't have carpets downstairs.

- ⚴ Store important belongings upstairs (or ensure they are easy to bring upstairs in the case of an alert).

- ⚴ Find out about local services that can clean up after a flood, especially drying-out services, and see what advice they offer to reduce the possible damage.

Overheating risk

You may have already experienced hot summers and heatwaves but the projection from the Met Office is that our summers will get hotter. There are no simple tools to assess your home's individual level of risk but you can learn from previous summers what the potential issues are for you.

A relatively simple way to assess this is to count up the risk factors in your home as I detailed in Chapter 3. Here are some more aspects to consider when assessing your own home:

1. **Build date.** Since 2000 building regulations have concentrated on insulation but have overlooked the risk of overheating. So if your home was built after 2000 you may be more at risk. There is also a risk with some pre-1900 homes that have solid walls and allow the sun's heat to transmit to the inside of a home.

2. **Whether you are in a 'hot' or 'cool' region of the UK.** Using the central summer overheating projections the following regions will be hot or not so hot (ie remain cool enough) in the future:

Region	Hot or cool?
Thames Valley	Hot
Severn Valley, South, South-East, South-West England	Hot
Midlands, East Anglia, East Pennines, West Pennines	Hot
North-West, North-East England, Borders	Cool
Wales, Northern Ireland, East/West Scotland	Cool
North-East Scotland, Highland, Western Isles	Cool
Orkney	Cool
Shetland	Cool

3. **Whether you live in a flat or apartment.** As flats can't always achieve full ventilation you may be at higher risk of overheating.

4. **Your home's aspect.** If you live in a flat and it is 'single aspect', ie there is only one external wall, then you are at even more risk of overheating. This is because even if you open the windows, there is no possibility of cross-ventilation.

5. **Whether you have communal heating.** You'll know if you have a communal heating system in your home – and this puts you at higher risk of overheating.

6. **Whether you live in an urban heat island.** This is difficult to assess but for our work we take a high density of dwellings as an indicator. First you have to look up which lower super output area (LSOA) your postcode is in (geoportal.statistics. gov.uk/datasets/postcode-to-output-area-to-lower-layer-super-output-area-to-middle-layer-super-output-area-to-

local-authority-district-august-2021-lookup-in-the-uk/ about), then look up the population in your LSOA and its area (ons.gov.uk/peoplepopulationandcommunity/ populationandmigration/populationestimates/datasets/ lowersuperoutputareapopulationdensity). Once you know the population and the area use this formula to work out dwelling density:

    a. divide the population by the area in km^2

    b. then divide that answer by 2.3 to estimate dwellings

    c. then divide that answer by 100 to get dwellings per hectare.

If it is above 46, this is a high dwelling density area and may be susceptible to the urban heat island effect.

If you look at the risk factors above and count them up for your home, you can come to a rough calculation for your risk of overheating. As a guide:

⌃ 1–2 risk factors = low risk of overheating

⌃ 3–4 risk factors = medium risk of overheating

⌃ 5–6 risk factors = high risk of overheating.

So, for example, if you live in a single aspect flat in a high dwelling density area in the south-east of England and have communal heating, you have a high number of risk factors. Of course, this isn't a full assessment, as whoever built your home may well have put mitigating factors in place to reduce the risks. For example, some builders go beyond building regulations and install background extraction ventilation. Not only does this extract impure air and condensation but it helps exhaust hot internal air.

For people who want to do detailed calculations the options are:

⅄ Appendix P of the SAP methodology (available at bre. co.uk/filelibrary/SAP/2012/SAP-2012_9-92.pdf). This is not for the faint hearted. Plus, it does not take into account future summer temperatures and omits a major risk factor – communal heating pipes.

⅄ CIBSE dynamic simulation modelling. This is costly and you need to get a qualified assessor to do it.

Some homes also have external shutters or brise soleil shading, which helps to reduce the amount of sun getting into the home. External planting also helps with summer cooling and a deciduous tree by the windows that face the sun can help. The leaves offer shading during the summer but will drop off in the autumn to allow daylight in. Another way to adapt your home is to have white exteriors that reflect the heat. If you do experience overheating in your home and you haven't yet made the changes above, there are still some steps you can take to reduce overheating:

⅄ Reduce internal gains – switch off lights and other equipment that generates heat.

⅄ Keep windows and curtains closed during the hottest parts of the day to prevent hot air getting in.

⅄ Open windows overnight when it is normally cooler to let any accumulated hot air out. However, this can sometimes be an issue if people are worried about crime, poor air quality or noise.

⅄ If ventilation systems are in place in your home, ensure they are switched on.

⅄ Use fans to make a breeze.

⅄ Drink plenty of cool fluids (non-alcoholic).

Biodiversity

As outlined in Chapter 3, one of the big threats to our food security as well as our mental wellbeing is the threat to biodiversity. So what can we do to improve biodiversity in our immediate environment? If you have a garden, then this is a great opportunity to green it as much as possible. There is no single metric that combines all aspects of biodiversity, so it's difficult to see if you have hit a sustainable target or not. That said, I remember reading a brochure in Germany that recommended setting aside between 5 and 9 per cent of your garden area for composting. Someone had clearly worked that one out carefully, so it doesn't seem a bad metric to use.

In my consultancy work we quantify biodiversity by the amount of biomass growing above ground. This tends to correlate with the good things that a biodiverse garden can offer but, like many metrics, it's not perfect, because someone could have lots of plants growing above ground but have used weedkiller to clear the ground before growing them. In this case, although the garden might look biodiverse, if there is only a limited range of cultivated plants they won't attract a larger variety of species. However, more growing matter is still better than a completely paved-over garden. On a related point, by removing the weeds and wild flowers you are removing plants that might be more attractive to native insects.

If you have control of a garden, however small, you might want to consider including some of the following:

- Edible and native species. As strange as it might sound, letting rampant native species fight it out for the best shading, sunlight or soil type will create a naturally biodiverse framework for the garden, as the right plant will naturally thrive in the right area. This in turn will attract a wide variety of insects and other wildlife.

⅄ As per the German calculations, set aside 5–9 per cent of the garden space for a compost area. This is for the compost heaps and the space around them for working. Compost is vital for biodiversity, as it not only improves soil structure and helps to increase water retention for your plants but provides food for decomposers. These can be soil invertebrates like earthworms or plants such as fungi that specialise in breaking down plant material. The more decomposers you have in your garden, the more birds and mammals you will attract that feed off the decomposers.

⅄ Keep paving to a minimum – a network of stepping stone paths that are kept strimmed is ideal. Strimmings can go in the compost area.

⅄ Change your idea of what looks pretty. A wild hedgerow or forest undergrowth looks just as nice as a pristine, well-kept garden, so think about whether you need non-native inedible flowers or whether you can encourage nature to take its course.

⅄ Consider these plants, which will establish well in most gardens and create lots of biodiversity:

✧ rosemary and bay

✧ oregano/marjoram – these grow wild in the UK

✧ mint – again, this grows wild and is great for Moroccan-style mint tea and tabbouleh

✧ Jerusalem artichoke – these are incredibly easy to grow and will colonise most gardens

✧ nasturtiums – these are easy to grow and the leaves and flowers are edible

✧ brambles for blackberries

✧ nettles – these can not only be eaten but can be used to make all sorts of things due to their strong stems

♦ rhubarb – this needs very little care and rhubarb can be used in many recipes, not just crumble

♦ runner beans, chard and courgettes – these all produce bountiful crops with little effort.

It's worth remembering that the plants listed above do not need weedkillers, insecticides, herbicides or other chemicals to thrive. Any garden with these elements will be a haven for insects, birds (if you include bird feeders you will get even more) and other wildlife.

For more authoritative information on creating a wildlife-friendly garden the RSPB offers great advice (see rspb.org.uk/birds-and-wildlife/advice/gardening-for-wildlife/creating-a-wildlife-friendly-garden):

1. Create the right habitats, eg fill borders with flowering plants and shrubs.

2. Provide somewhere safe for birds to breed and shelter, eg birdboxes.

3. Provide foraging and feeding spaces, eg berry bushes.

4. Think sustainably, eg avoid peat.

If you don't have a garden and you still want to apply some of these ideas, you could either try and get an allotment or do a deal with a neighbour who has a neglected garden where you tend the garden in return for keeping the produce (and making a new friend!).

Air quality

Needless to say, we breathe the air around us, and how polluted it is depends on our own actions as well as the actions of others in our area. So we can a) make a fair contribution to reducing air pollution overall; and b) try to improve the air quality in our own homes.

You can look up the air quality for your region on the Defra Air Quality website (uk-air.defra.gov.uk/data/DAQI-regional-data). Historic Daily Air Quality Index (DAQI) data is only available at a regional basis. If you wanted to see the annual data then it's a bit of downloading and spreadsheet work. This data is for inorganic pollutants not organic ones like viruses.

How we can make a fair contribution

⅄ **Energy-efficient homes.** As described above, burning gas, oil, coal or wood to heat our homes or the hot water in our homes not only causes CO_2 emissions but also localised air pollutants with funny names like NOx (nitrogen oxides), PM (particulate matter), SOx (sulphur dioxide) and O_3 (ozone). All of these affect our air quality and respiratory systems.

⅄ **Efficient transport**. A big chunk of local air pollution comes from transport, which is why you often see pollution maps located near roads. We can all make our own contribution by ensuring our transport is as sustainable as possible.

⅄ **Minimising bonfires and fireworks.** I don't want to be a spoilsport (after all, this book is about maximising happiness for everyone) but consider your neighbours when lighting fires or setting off fireworks.

Indoor air quality

⅄ **Ventilation.** Pollutants inside the home are best controlled by ventilating your home. This can be achieved either by opening windows or using the ventilation systems in your home. Unless you are lucky enough to have an MVHR system, this will mostly be unfiltered and cold, new air, so if the outdoor air is worse than the indoor air then it's probably best not to do this. How do you know if the outdoor air is worse? If the DAQI value is between 1 and 6, the health advice is that everyone can enjoy the outdoors. If the DAQI is 7 or above, then people with respiratory disorders are advised to reduce activities and exertion outdoors. So a DAQI of 7 or above would be a time to not open windows. The International Well Building Institute has a building standard (the WELL standard, available at standard.wellcertified.com) that deals with multiple aspects of wellbeing inside of buildings. It recommends that windows should not be opened:

If the outdoor air measurement system indicates that outdoor air either (i) exceeds ozone levels of 51 ppb or PM_{10} levels of 50 µg/m³; (ii) has a temperature of 8°C [15°F] above or below set indoor temperature; or (iii) has a relative humidity above 60…

These correspond roughly with World Health Organization limits. Another step you can take to know if the outdoor air quality is or is going to be poor is to sign up for air pollution alerts at uk-air.defra.gov.uk/subscribe. You will then receive an email if a poor air quality limit is predicted to be exceeded.

⋏ **Low VOCs.** Volatile organic compounds are used in the manufacture of many household products. Over time they are slowly released from those products into the indoor air and, according to the WELL building standard, are associated with leukaemia, childhood asthma and other respiratory disorders. They also note that VOC levels can be five times higher indoors than outdoors. Ventilation is key to getting rid of these pollutants, but even better is to reduce the amount of them in your home in the first place.

According to WELL, the worst products for VOCs are interior paints and coatings; interior adhesives and sealants; floor coverings (including carpets); insulation (both thermal and soundproofing); furniture and furnishings. There isn't a ubiquitous, widely agreed logo or standard labelling system to help consumers choose between products at the moment, so you will need to do your own research. The easiest way to do this is to ask the seller of the product – and if more and more of us ask then it may prompt the manufacturing industries to get their house in order. Asthma UK has a list of recommendations for maintaining good indoor air quality, ranging from getting carpet sellers to unroll carpets before they deliver to using air purifiers (asthma.org.uk/ advice/triggers/indoor-environment).

⅄ **Condensation.** This is caused by air that contains high levels of moisture. In the same way that you can dissolve more sugar in warm water compared to cold water, more water can be 'dissolved' in warm air than cold air. When this water-laden warm air comes into contact with cold surfaces, the air cools down and cannot hold the water any longer. It then condenses out of the air to form moisture on those surfaces. When the moisture is in contact for too long with those surfaces, mould growth can occur and spores from this mould are released into indoor air causing air quality issues. Prevention is ideal (for example, avoid excess moisture by drying clothes outside when you can) and ventilation is critical too. This is a highly contentious issue, particularly in rented properties where the responsibility for condensation problems (homeowner or tenant) is much disputed (Housing Ombudsman Service 2021). But there are a few things you can do that overlap with other environmental impact reductions:

✧ Make your home energy efficient. An energy-efficient home is cheaper to keep warm, so there are fewer cold surfaces. But remember to include ventilation when insulating and installing double glazing.

✧ Have showers instead of baths. Again, this means that less steam is introduced into the air, which means there is less to condense. Opting for an aerated shower head as suggested in Chapter 5 will help with this.

✧ Keep lids on saucepans. This not only saves energy but reduces the amount of condensation in the home.

If you want to monitor moisture levels, you can buy humidity meters quite cheaply. These record relative humidity (RH) as a percentage. According to the WELL building standard the ideal level is between 30 and 50 per cent RH.

Future technology and developments

In the next few years there will be great advances in technology when it comes to air quality. Someone called me just the other day to tell me about an ozone device he was manufacturing. The device manufactures ozone from the air at low, safe levels and then introduces it into indoor spaces. Why is this a good idea? At low levels, ozone acts like bleach and will therefore destroy organic compounds in the air. It can also help destroy viruses, which the ozone then breaks back down to oxygen. This is not yet a widespread technology but I wonder if this could be installed in ventilation ductwork where it exists. It could then be turned on when indoor air quality is poor or if there is increased risk from viruses. This is an example of a great opportunity in the MVHR sector as it becomes more widespread.

When we learn to measure our security (see Chapter 3), we can then start to manage it. Knowing our risk of flooding, overheating or exposure to poor air quality can enable us to take steps to increase our protection from these negative effects. On page 142 I will look at how to rate these changes in the home to add to the happiness matrix at the end of Chapter 7.

Now let's look at how we affect our own happiness by our activities and interactions with the world outside the home.

Chapter 7
Out and about

I've already looked at what we do inside the home and where we can make changes that will protect our overall security. But what about outside the home? This is where some of our most impactful behaviour takes place. The first of these is travel.

Transport

Nowhere in Maslow's framework does it say that travel is an essential biological need. And yet transport is responsible for roughly a third of the UK's annual CO_2 emissions. Does our non-basic happiness depend on our ability to take holidays? For some people, maybe. But aside from that, if we want to obtain our food, build our homes and extract our water, we do need to move around. I'll expand on how we can do this in Chapter 8 but for now we need to know that finding sustainable forms of transport is essential for reducing our environmental impacts which in turn puts the supply of our basic needs at risk.

The overall plan for domestic transport in the UK is to move to active travel (eg walking and cycling for those who can) and to decarbonise exhaust emissions from cars and public transport (Department for Transport 2021). Decarbonising tailpipe emissions will mean electric cars, buses and trains. To some extent, using hydrogen to fuel our public transport is in the mix too but is unlikely to be for cars so is outside the scope of this book. Also outside the scope of this book but good to know is that there are plans to decarbonise the way we deliver our goods and aviation. Decarbonising freight will be via electric and hydrogen-based modes of transport and switching from road to train. Aviation emissions will be offset in the short term but in the long term it is likely we will switch to sustainable aviation fuel. This is yet to be researched but is likely to include biofuels, electricity and maybe hydrogen.

On a personal level, we have to travel around to satisfy our basic needs. I'll interpret that loosely to mean the following:

1. Getting food. Luckily, in the UK we don't need to travel to get water as it is delivered to our homes. That said, I do see people collecting water from local springs and wells where I live to avoid using tap water. Just for clarity, these people prefer to do this instead of using mains water.

2. Getting to work and back. For many of us transport is vital to allow us to earn money to pay for our basic needs.

3. Getting to school. Education is key to the security of our basic needs.

During the pandemic it became clear that it is possible for many people (although not all) to work and learn from home. This would certainly reduce transport emissions for those who normally travel by motor vehicle but it would also mean more use of heaters and kettles at home compared to the potentially more efficient heaters and hot water at the office. However, if your employer is happy and your home is very efficient – perhaps you generate your own electricity – then this is a more environmentally efficient option. It may not be a preference for everyone, though. If you started a new job or your home is not blessed with a suitable study and seating, then perhaps working from home is not ideal. The jury is out on what will emerge but at least we know that, for many, it's an option. However, we must remember that we are social beings (note the third level on Maslow's hierarchy), so removing physical meetings and replacing them with video conferencing might have other implications for wellbeing.

Another way of reducing transport is by receiving our basic goods such as food and the products we need to maintain our home by post. The most obvious example of this is receiving food deliveries. However, again the dilemma emerges about whether or not this is more environmentally friendly. If you normally drive to the food shops in a fossil fuel car then receiving food deliveries saves you burning those fossil fuels. But this means that the supermarket delivery van is now using more fossil fuels. Are their carefully planned delivery routes more energy efficient? And are they switching to more and more sustainable forms of delivery vehicle? It's a fast-changing world and I haven't seen any conclusive reports on the matter. Industry-led reports certainly seem to suggest that deliveries are better for the environment but there are lots of factors to take into account. I'd suggest that you use the option most convenient to you and if it happens to be by fossil fuel car then consider making changes to make that more environmentally friendly (see later in this section). You might also want to consider the environmental impact of the products you buy, but that will be discussed later in this chapter.

So how can we travel more sustainably? Perhaps the most environmentally friendly method is walking. This is a great way to travel short distances and keep fit at the same time. Walking burns off around 300 calories an hour and the NHS recommendation is to do 10,000 steps a day. So why not use these steps to satisfy your basic needs, if you are able to? 10,000 steps is around 5 miles or 8 km so you can certainly plan your trips based on that metric. There are many ways to incorporate a bit of walking into your everyday trips. One of my favourites is this: if you take the bus to work, get off one stop earlier and walk the rest of the way.

It can also be a great way to start the day. I was lucky enough for a few years to work within a 30-minute walk from my home. I have always had a walking mentality and wouldn't take the bus or train anyway for such a short distance. With a typical commuter mentality I worked out the most direct route that took me along busy roads and built-up areas. Then, after one particularly indulgent Christmas, I put on a bit of weight and I remembered a tip about choosing a slightly longer route just to get more steps in. So I adjusted my route by an extra 10 minutes to take me through a beautiful park. Every morning and evening on my walking commute I was totally immersed in nature in this park and saw everything from deer to woodpeckers to rabbits and carp in the ponds. It was not only good for the environment and my health but a great way to start and finish the day. Luckily, I can still walk to my new office and I still choose a slightly longer 'green' route.

Cycling is another great physical exercise and one that is certainly being promoted as part of the future of transport in the UK. We can expect to see more infrastructure dedicated to bike riding, making it a safer and more convenient mode of transport. At the moment cycling isn't for everyone and some people have concerns about road safety and the weather. That said, there are plenty of road safety courses you can take to boost your confidence (see bikeability.org.uk/find-cycle-training). On a personal level, when I lived in London, I felt more secure cycling the streets there than in the country lanes that surround my current home. The traffic was slower and more used to cyclists. You can find cycle-friendly routes via the Sustrans website (sustrans.org.uk), Ordnance Survey maps or even by looking up cycle routes on Google Maps.

If the weather is an issue for you then why not choose to only cycle on nice weather days? Every little helps. Again, when I lived in London it rained far less than people think. In the south-east there are fewer rainy days than in other parts of the country and I cycled from the suburbs to central London for two years and only had to don my waterproofs about 10 times during the whole period. Cycling also burns off at least 400 calories per hour, so it's good for your health too.

To make things easier, you can ensure that you have good cycle storage for your bike. I built one in a previous house inspired by something called the Code for Sustainable Homes (DLUHC 2010). The main things to remember about bike storage are that it should:

- ⚑ be big enough to get the bike in and out easily
- ⚑ have easy access to the road
- ⚑ be secure
- ⚑ be sheltered from the weather.

Apart from walking and cycling, all other options involve burning some kind of fossil fuel (at the moment). However, we can still make choices. Here is a list of CO_2 per distance travelled according to the Defra (2021) figures (ie not the manufacturers' claims). Note that CO_2e means CO_2 equivalent. Other exhaust gases, such as nitrous oxides, also have a greenhouse gas effect and their impacts are captured by using this metric:

- ⚑ Car – medium diesel: 0.16496 kg CO_2e per km driven (but remember that diesel cars are associated with other forms of air pollution).
- ⚑ Car – medium petrol: 0.18785 kg CO_2e per km driven.
- ⚑ Car – medium hybrid: 0.10957 kg CO_2e per km driven. You still fill up a hybrid with petrol, which runs an engine, which charges an electric battery. The reason it's more efficient than a pure petrol car is that the engine is fine tuned to work at one output level and the battery also gets charged when

you apply the brakes. You cannot plug in this car to charge the battery. The benefit is that there is absolutely no range anxiety with current infrastructure.

⌃ Car – medium plug-in hybrid: 0.09097 kg CO_2e per km driven. These are a halfway house between a hybrid and a fully electric. The engine and battery are sized accordingly. You can either fill with petrol or charge or a combination of the two. Anecdotally, owners either haven't got into the habit of putting these on electric charge yet or haven't got the facility to install a charger. Hence their CO_2 emissions are not far off a hybrid.

⌃ Car – medium battery electric: 0.05254 kg CO_2e per km driven. These are pure battery and electric motor-based and can only be 'refilled' with electricity. The ranges of newer models are very similar to their fossil fuel equivalents. More and more infrastructure is being developed for these cars and after a bit of getting used to, there's no real impingement on your life. For example, you can charge in car parks while you go shopping or while you are having a coffee break on longer journeys.

⌃ Medium petrol motorbike: 0.1009 kg CO_2 per km travelled.

⌃ Regular taxi: 0.14876 kg CO_2 per passenger km travelled but slightly higher for black cabs.

⌃ Average bus: 0.10227 kg CO_2e per passenger km travelled.

⌃ National rail: 0.03549 kg CO_2e per passenger km travelled.

There are no Defra statistics for electric bikes but some research suggests that a 500 Wh battery will get you 33 miles (Cycling UK 2022). Assuming a 100 per cent charger efficiency from grid electricity to the battery, this calculates at 0.00219 kgs CO_2e per passenger kilometre travelled.

It is unlikely you'll be flying or using sea travel to meet your basic needs so the environmental impacts of these are discussed in the next chapter.

The list above shows the CO_2 impact of travel but there are other environmental impacts from driving such as brake dust from disc brakes and particularly the impact of manufacturing the cars in the first place. Ultimately the mode you choose will also depend on what you can afford and overall suitability to your needs (eg how far you regularly drive and how many people or how much stuff you need to carry). I would encourage you to include the environmental impacts in your list of decision factors when seeking your next mode of transport.

If you already have a car and are not ready to change just yet, here's a list of fuel-efficient driving techniques that will help you now and when you get a new car. Again, there are other far more detailed resources out there (see energysavingtrust.org.uk/advice/efficient-driving/, for example), but here are some steps you can take for now:

1. Drive smoothly. By anticipating the road and maintaining distance behind other drivers you can avoid heavy accelerating and decelerating, which is more fuel efficient.

2. Shift up a gear early. This allows your engine to run at its most efficient revs.

3. Avoid excessive speeds. For example, at 75 mph a car uses around 18 per cent more fuel than at 60 mph.

4. Switch off the engine. If you are going to be stationary for more than a minute switch the engine off.

5. Watch your tyre pressure. Keep your tyre pressure as per the manufacturer's instructions as low tyre pressures lead to inefficient driving.

6. Remove roof racks. These add extra drag on your car, so remove them if you are not using them.

7. Rethink air conditioning. These systems can use up to 5 per cent extra fuel, so if you can, use the windows more than the air con.

Buying power

Everything we buy has, at some point, been extracted from our environment. From the minerals and fossil fuels extracted from the earth's crust to make our metals and other materials to the commodities we grow for our food, pharmaceutical and other uses, it all comes from the earth and the extraction processes all have an environmental impact.

At first glance it may be easy to say 'stop buying stuff' to reduce our environmental impacts. But the truth is we have a biological need for certain items. We need food and we need shelter. We need to be able to travel to get these things as we can't just sit in one place and acquire them like a tree. For sure, there are things that we don't need to buy and we will deal with these in the next chapter but for this chapter we'll recognise that we do need to acquire certain basics. And as we currently live in a capitalist economy (but please take a look at Chapter 9), we need to buy most of these items to satisfy our basic and security needs.

So the trick is to buy the things we need and have no environmental impact. This is made harder for us consumers because there is no easy way to judge whether something we're buying is ethical or has low environmental impact. There is not even a standard definition of what is ethical or sustainable or low environmental impact. In fact, some manufacturers claim their products are ethical but on further investigation it turns out that they are just greenwashing.

Despite this confusion it is clear that the current system of prioritising unlimited growth over environmental protection and human wellbeing is not sustainable. In fact, the United Nations even states that transforming economic growth with a specific emphasis on human wellbeing is essential if we want to keep our impacts manageable (SHIFT 2021).

One study suggests that ethical consumer spend in the UK is £122 billion a year (Ethical Consumer 2021). Given that the UK consumer economy is worth around £1,257 billion that means that only 10 per cent of our spending is ethical (ONS 2022c). Clearly a lot more is needed both from manufacturers and from regulation so that we can have a consistent definition of ethical spending. There are signs of change though. The same report that gave us the £122 billion figure also highlights that 'ethical spending' is a growth industry and has increased by 113 per cent since 2010. Hopefully this growth will continue and provide an incentive for all manufacturers to become ethical.

In the meantime, it's helpful to understand more about the impact of what we buy.

Embodied carbon

As an indication of the trouble with defining 'ethical' and the challenge of actually putting a figure on it, here's something we did in my consultancy practice. Many of our clients were keen to know more about the embodied carbon in the materials they use. Embodied carbon is the term for all the carbon emissions associated with the production of certain materials and goods, over and on top of the carbon the product itself produces. For example, concrete production involves:

- the extraction of raw cement from the ground, which produces calcium carbonate and uses diesel-operated machinery
- heating those materials in a cement kiln using fossil fuels
- carbon emissions from the dissociation of calcium carbonate into cement

- energy used in extraction of aggregates

- energy used in the mixing of concrete.

These can be summed and apportioned to get an embodied carbon figure for the UK in 2021 of 131.76 kg CO_2e per tonne of concrete used. Similar sums can be done for other materials.

The calculations for this aren't particularly complex but getting hold of the input data is normally a lot of work. To help some of our clients work out their embodied carbon figures, we looked at some typical values. For example, many of our housing association clients had already asked about the embodied carbon of construction materials. Not only is this interesting for understanding complete carbon emissions from their operations but it is also a factor (among many others) in deciding between refurbishing a home or demolishing and rebuilding it.

Discussions over embodied carbon often revolve around academic studies involving life cycle analyses. Fortunately, a government-backed methodology for material use makes things a little easier. We took the opportunity to test out the methodology for homes and here's what we found.

First off, we needed to know the amount of materials used. As this was just an initial experiment with the methodology, we used some waste statistics as a proxy for estimating the amount of materials going into a retrofit/repair. The assumption was that whatever has come out of a house in the form of waste has been replaced by new material. We then added on an amount for packaging. For a new-build home, we simply estimated the weight of the materials in a home based on the volume of the building elements in a very simplified unit.

Then we apply the relevant embodied carbon figures, with the following results:

- Retrofit/repairs averaged around 0.009 tonnes CO_2e per home managed.

⅄ Building a new home incurred around 8.4 tonnes CO_2e per home built.

This had a number of implications:

⅄ When we compare this figure to the previous calculations for housing stock and operational carbon emissions that we have done for scores of social landlords, embodied carbon amounts to about 6 per cent of total emissions.

⅄ If older, energy-inefficient homes are demolished and replaced with a net zero new-build, the carbon payback is something like three years.

⅄ These figures could start to influence discussions on materiality of embodied carbon for compliance reporting.

In any case, now that the methodologies are available, it should be easier for organisations to engage with their supply chain to a) gain the relevant CO_2 figures; and b) encourage them to make CO_2 reductions in construction materials, even if that means they in turn need to engage with their own supply chain.

Regardless of whether embodied carbon in construction materials is 'material' or not, it is crucial for organisations to engage with their supply chains on environmental issues. Once the supply chain knows that organisations are interested, they are more likely to respond to the challenge.

The point of relating this story is to illustrate that, although it is possible to calculate environmental impacts of different products, the ways of doing it are data hungry and too time consuming for day-to-day decision making. The example above only looked at one environmental issue (carbon) for one product (concrete). For something like a mobile phone, there are lots of different materials and lots of different environmental issues.

In an ideal world, perhaps the UK could organise itself such that everything that was up for sale had excellent environmental credentials and anything with bad credentials simply wouldn't be allowed to be imported or manufactured in this country. Alas, we don't yet live in an ideal world, so the next best thing we can do is look at eco labels.

The labelling of goods for the purpose of working out how environmentally friendly they are is fraught with difficulties. How do we know what to believe? Let's take a look at a range of goods and some of the labelling attached.

Food

There is no doubt that there are compelling cases for eating less meat but I guess it will take a few generations before the world has transitioned over and certainly not before the 2050 climate change targets come into view. Besides, it's not my job to tell you to become vegetarian or vegan. That said, the food industry is investing heavily in finding plant-based alternatives to meat as a protein source for us all. So it looks as if a plant-based diet is part of the future and as such it's worth giving it a go. I enjoy meat-free meals on a regular basis and I can imagine a world in the future where far less meat is consumed. There doesn't seem to be any biological barrier to it either: although the meat industry claims that meat is the only source of essential B12 vitamins, the Vegan Society argues that B12 can be derived from non-meat-based micro-organisms and taken as supplements. My biology isn't good enough to declare either argument right or wrong but perhaps time will tell.

As well as securing our source of food, it's also important to secure our physical health. And if we are to secure our health so that we can continue to satisfy our needs then we need to eat healthily. There are hundreds of books on this but if you want to measure healthy eating here are a couple of guidelines from the NHS:

⚠ Five a day – eat a variety of five portions of fruit and vegetables a day. This will largely give you the variety of vitamins and other nutrients your body needs.

⚠ Calories – as a guide men need around 2,500 kcal a day and women need about 2,000 kcal a day to maintain a healthy body weight. This does vary between people but is a useful benchmark.

Whether we eat meat or not, we as householders can take steps to consume sustainably sourced food. The challenge is to unscramble the plethora of labels attached to our food and work out what is – and isn't – ethically produced.

Rainforest Alliance

You may have seen the Rainforest Alliance frog label on packets of coffee and tea. Their assessment scheme covers a wide range of environmental and social impacts. I took a deeper look at their energy efficiency as a barometer for how robust the scheme is. One of the things I found was that, although implementing energy efficiency measures is a mandatory requirement to gain the Rainforest Alliance label, actually declaring and working towards a target greenhouse gas emission rate is voluntary. So there is no need to achieve a certain amount of CO_2 per tonne of tea to gain certification. This seems quite common among agricultural labels.

I also took a closer look to see if there was anything in the Alliance's guidelines about plastic in teabags but there is nothing. Plastic is used in teabags to seal the edge of the bags so that they don't fall apart in our cups or teapots. This means that if we put used teabags in our compost bins, we are introducing plastic into our soil. There are moves from tea bag manufacturers to phase in polylactic acid (PLA) plastic. Some producers have already done so and others have plans to implement it in the next few years. PLA is manufactured from crops such as corn and cassava and is fully biodegradable. Sadly, there is no label that shows which teabags have PLA and which don't but if you are inclined to research it most manufacturers indicate their status on the issue on their websites.

Fairtrade International

This is another established label that has its origins more in welfare for agricultural workers than in environmental protection. However, although the origin of the scheme was about worker welfare and fair prices for commodities it does now have a climate change standard. This encourages smallholders to commit to CO_2-reducing projects and the amount of CO_2 saved is logged and certified as a Fairtrade Carbon Credit. Companies and individuals elsewhere can buy these credits to offset their own carbon emissions and proceeds go to the smallholder. This is an offsetting scheme and carbon offsetting is fraught with issues but hopefully with an organisation with Fairtrade's reputation behind it, the money does go to the smallholders who can use it for CO_2-reducing projects.

Marine Stewardship Council (MSC)

This is another respectable organisation, this time concentrating on fish. You may have seen the blue label on fish products. MSC mainly focuses on making sure that fish are harvested from places where fish stocks are sustainable (ie they aren't on the brink of collapse). However, the standards also include minimising environmental impact, although while this covers impacts such as the loss of fishing nets into the environment, it does not cover other effects such as reducing carbon emissions from boat engines.

Soil Association

This is the main label for organic food products. The focus is on ensuring that organic methods have been used to produce the products, so no artificial fertilisers or artificial additives and good animal welfare. As with other food labels there are no targets to reduce greenhouse gases but it is still a legitimate label for other environmental impacts.

Red Tractor

This is a joint scheme between farmers and the food industry and focuses on animal welfare rather than any direct environmental impacts. For example, the pork standard doesn't list environmental impacts, although the fruit and vegetable standard does mention 'minimising' impact.

Products for the home

Shopping ethically isn't just about food. We can also improve our security by thinking about the other products we buy. And as for food, there are a number of labels that can help us decide what is environmentally friendly and what is less so. Here are a few to think about.

Forest Stewardship Council (FSC)

This scheme is for timber and timber products. It focuses on welfare of farm workers and environmentally sound forest management techniques. Their impact reports have some good data. For example, forest fires were less common in FSC forests than in other forests. Most wood products for sale in the UK are either FSC or PEFC (a similar label) certified – in fact, I've heard some people say that it's harder to find uncertified wood than certified.

BES 6001

For materials other than wood, BES 6001 is an all-encompassing standard for both workers' welfare and environmental protection. It is quite a loose standard and talks about minimising impacts rather than setting numerical targets but it's better than nothing and has the potential to evolve into something even more robust. DIY shops are responding to public pressure to develop clear eco labelling so that consumers know what we are buying, so keep up the pressure.

A-rated white goods

We've already seen the A–G rating on EPC certificates for homes. A similar system exists for white goods such as fridges and washing machines. These are regulated labels and describe the energy efficiency of the goods (as well as noise, water efficiency and volume). However, they give no other indication of how ethically the product was made or the other environmental implications of using the item.

That said, these ratings are a success story. When they originally came out, fridge manufacturers were typically 'D' rated. With the introduction of the labelling scheme, manufacturers began competing to make ever more energy-efficient white goods, so much so that higher levels than 'A' had to be invented, so we started to see A+, A++ and A+++ products. In 2021 the system was reset so that the top rank is once again A-rated and items that were previously rated A++ are now D rated. Hopefully the manufacturers will rise to the challenge again and strive to produce more and more A-rated items.

Car tyres

The last time I replaced my car tyres I was pleasantly surprised to see the familiar A–G rating available to help me make my choice. The label rates the fuel efficiency of using a particular tyre. Choosing an A-rated tyre over a G-rated tyre can save 6 litres of fuel for every 1,000 km driven (RAC 2019).

Cleanright

You can find this label on many cleaning products. It has gone through a few name changes but seems a reasonable scheme as companies with responsible credentials set it up. It signifies a more environmentally friendly way to clean.

Ecolabel paper

If you are buying paper for your printer there is an Ecolabel mark, a European Union-governed scheme which signifies that the producer has a rigorous environmental management system in place. You can also buy FSC paper products.

Blaue Engel

Still on printers, this label focuses on printer cartridges. Many of us have become used to disposing of spent cartridges responsibly – but what about the new ones we buy? Blaue Engel is the only scheme I've come across that signifies environmentally safe manufacturing processes. It is not on all cartridges, although it does examine the manufacturing process before certifying.

Ethical clothes and fast fashion

There has been a lot of focus on the environmental impact of clothes recently and rightly so. Not only does clothes manufacturing have huge environmental impacts but we have seen some of the awful cases of poor working conditions that workers have to endure to produce the clothes we wear. There is no doubt that warm clothing is one of our basic needs, as are safety clothes that protect us from harm. That said, a lot of clothes retail is for fashion rather than to satisfy our basic needs. So taking a sustainable approach to buying clothes while still satisfying our needs is essential.

I'm the last person anyone would describe as a fashion guru

and I tend only to buy something if the previous item of clothing has fallen to bits or I've forgotten something on holiday. But there are a few things you can do to remain fashionable while taking care of the planet:

- Do an audit of your current wardrobe and think about which clothes you wear the most and why. This will give you an idea of the type of items you actually wear rather than buying clothes you like because you think you will wear them. I have developed a mental checklist that I include in my buying decisions. One of the questions I ask is whether the item can be washed in the washing machine at normal temperatures. If it requires anything other than that, I'm reluctant to buy it.

- If fashion is your thing, then try and gain an idea of long-term trends. Fashion designers think a few years ahead, so as long as you follow these themes rather than short-lived fads your clothes will remain fashionable and you won't have to buy this year's trend just to stay with it.

At the time of writing I'm not aware of any ubiquitous labelling scheme that determines whether an item is sustainable or not but there are resources out there to help influence your decision. Here's a list from Friends of the Earth (friendsoftheearth.uk/climate/live-sustainably-how-be-conscious-consumer):

- Buy better-made clothes and shoes. They may cost more upfront, but they'll be cheaper in the long run.

- Repair rather than replace clothes. This will lessen the load on your wallet and the planet.

- Buy and sell unwanted goods using websites like Shpock, Gumtree and eBay.

On that last point, one of my best clothing buys was from a charity shop, where I got a great quality waterproof jacket for about 10 per cent of the price it would have been new.

The above information is by no means an exhaustive list of labelling schemes and there are lots of different initiatives out there but they do take quite a bit of investigating to see if they are good and robust. Once I was working with a firm that operated an environmental management scheme (EMS) for businesses called ISO 14001. Their documents were all audited and correct and stated that they would monitor their carbon footprint on a quarterly basis. However, when I asked to see the quarterly carbon figures there was a long delay before I received them. I delved a bit deeper, only to find that the firm was having difficulty getting the data from their energy supplier. If their audited and approved EMS was working well there should not have been any delay.

In this way most of the labels I've seen are tick box schemes with a bit of judgement required by the assessor. They lack numerical targets that provide transparency to ensure that a measurable ideal is reached. Of course, there is plenty of criticism that labels don't go far enough. But a label is a good start and perhaps over time they will evolve into something that becomes even more robust.

These schemes are a business tool and like any other are open to abuse as well as being used in the manner intended. They can be a great framework to make a real difference, or they can be viewed as burdensome paperwork. In the end it all depends on the management commitment of the organisation involved.

Due to the complexity involved, I would like to see the government take the lead and detail a proper sustainability standard to ensure that any goods placed on the market in the UK comply. I've even thought of a scheme to manage the transition. The idea is that if we import goods from other places that don't have the same wellbeing record as us (as measured by the Maslow framework), then import duty is applied in proportion to the lack of wellbeing in that country. Collected duties are then given back to those countries as charity aid with the ring-fenced aim of improving wellbeing in those areas. Eventually those places will have 100 per cent wellbeing and their corresponding import duties will be nil.

Shop local

Sometimes where we shop is as important as what we buy. I've often seen 'locally sourced' as a description of a product to boost its environmental credentials. However, I'm not aware of any labels that can confirm or otherwise how locally sourced a product is. I stayed in a bed and breakfast where they described the breakfast as locally sourced. However, when we got there, we saw lots of shopping bags from a famous brand supermarket. So while to the B&B proprietor the bread was 'locally sourced' from the local supermarket, I have no idea about the credentials of the supply chain behind getting the bread to the supermarket in the first place. The reality is that when you make carbon calculations for products, transportation from the factory to the end consumer is often a small part of the overall carbon footprint. Most of the emissions come from making or using the product.

Of course, shopping locally can save carbon emissions but it's not clear cut whether it's always more environmentally friendly. Assuming that the trader who sells the product keeps the money in the local economy, there can be local economic benefits and it can keep high street shops open. But whether or not shopping locally is a long-term benefit to our overall wellbeing is a grey area.

Animal welfare

It may not seem directly obvious why creating good animal welfare is a necessity for human wellbeing. After all, if we are going to slaughter the animal anyway, what's in it for us to be concerned about its welfare? Most people (me included) in the UK don't like the thought of treating animals badly during their lifetime but we are happy enough to let someone else slaughter them and prepare them for our tables. How does this fit into the Maslow framework? How does the welfare of animals affect our human biology? I've not seen anything definitive on this but there are some emerging points:

- ⅄ Antibiotic use – antibiotics are often used to treat sick animals but they also result in weight gain, which means that farmers who sell meat by the kilogram are incentivised to give more antibiotics. Campaigners also note that if animals weren't kept in such confined spaces (as in factory farms) then diseases and illness spread would not be so rife and therefore antibiotics wouldn't be so necessary. In any case, overuse of antibiotics leads to ever more resistant strains of infectious bacteria, for which we eventually might not be able to develop antibiotics. This means that we humans will also be deprived of a vital medicine. This issue is recognised in the food standards above that are concerned with animal welfare.

- ⅄ Cross-species transfer of diseases (zoonotic diseases) – poorly looked-after animals may get diseases that eventually transfer to humans. Covid-19 is an example of a zoonotic disease.

I've also seen a few academic papers that link humans who perpetrate animal cruelty with cruelty to other humans but this doesn't seem to be an issue raised by animal welfare campaigners.

In any case I think there should be some clear messaging about animal welfare and the links to our own long-term wellbeing. If this doesn't happen then I fear that when the UK enters into trade deals with other countries that don't have the same welfare standards as us, we may see cheap meat on our shelves but at the price of our own long-term wellbeing.

Interestingly, the principles of animal welfare look pretty similar to Maslow's framework (FAWC 2009):

1. freedom from thirst and hunger (basic need)

2. freedom from discomfort by providing adequate shelter (basic need)

3. freedom from disease, pain, or injury (security need)

4. freedom from distress and fear (security need)

5. freedom to engage in natural behaviours (certainly social needs and maybe even esteem and self-actualisation needs).

Waste not, want not

In the UK we generate about 400 kg of waste per person per year. Around 45 per cent of it gets recycled and the rest is either landfilled or incinerated. That's 55 per cent of our resources wasted. What's more, most of the stuff we throw away has to be replaced, which means more new resources taken from our environment. It's probably not worth creating a metric to measure household waste, as you know how full your bins are when you put them out. But there are lots of steps you can take to reduce waste.

Of course, the best thing is not to buy so much in the first place. This will not only save you money but have the benefit of not cluttering up your home. If you are a retail therapy subscriber, it may be worth looking at Chapter 8 to see if there is anything else that might satisfy these needs.

This section isn't about putting a ban on buying things. We need food, products to maintain our homes, transport, etc – and the section above will give you some sustainable guidance on that. This is just a plea to make sure that if you do buy something, make sure you are doing so to satisfy a real need.

The UK authority on this is WRAP and their Recycle Now

action has loads of resources on waste reduction tips. I'm not going to note them all but here are a few that I've found helpful:

1. Install waste recycling bins. You can buy these as stand-alone bins now to replace any whole waste bins you may have, which means you won't lose space in your kitchen.

2. If you are having a new kitchen fitted then make sure recycling bins are included.

3. Cut the backs of envelopes or spare paper into A5 size and hold together with a bulldog clip to keep things neat (no need to be a messy recycler). This makes a useful notepad and I haven't had to buy notepaper for years. Anything smaller than A5 goes in the recycling bin (no need to be a hoarder either).

4. Use empty jam jars as drinking glasses.

5. Turn your external bin store into something attractive/ useful. I've made an external shelf under which I can put a recycling bin and on top of it is a large plant. It's a chance to get creative about your bin store while making sure it's accessible and usable.

6. Sell unwanted goods. The outlets and possibilities for this are endless. You will no doubt have heard of eBay and Gumtree but there is also Facebook Marketplace, Depop, Vinted and many others. It takes a little time to set up an account, write a description and research what price you might want to sell at (remember to base this on what people will pay, which may be very different from what you paid for it). Car boot sales are another option but they require an early start and of course you need a car. I've tried all of these and have sold many unwanted items. I've never had a bad experience and transactions have been very smooth. It's amazing what people will buy and what they use it for

– even broken goods can be sold for spares. I've found the benefits are manifold:

- ◇ You earn money.
- ◇ You save the planet's resources.
- ◇ You are giving other people the chance to enjoy those goods and it's cost effective for them.
- ◇ You'll get good training in marketing skills – always useful.
- ◇ If you've tried and cannot sell an item, you know that it genuinely is waste. This has helped me to make the decision between keeping something 'just in case' and disposing of it sustainably.

7. Repairing things is always fun. If the item is broken anyway, then you've really nothing to lose except a bit of labour in trying to repair it. I've always found it interesting to take things apart and see how they all work. And I've had loads of successes too. It also encourages you to get imaginative, especially with thin bits of plastic that are broken and hard to glue back together. I've often used screws and bits of wood with success. OK, the item isn't necessarily restored to its original status but the thing still works. And if you can't get to work again, at least you know it genuinely is waste.

8. If you can't be bothered to price something or don't think it's worth anything, then you can always give it away for free. Freecycle and Facebook Marketplace are good for that. At the very least, someone else is getting a benefit and you don't have the hassle of disposing of it. Marketplace also invites you to share your item with local Facebook groups.

9. Recycle all the waste you can. Your local authority will give you details on recycling opportunities either for bin

collections or where the local recycling centres (tips) are. Supermarkets have battery recycling boxes and DIY shops also take light bulbs.

10. Upcycling is popular and there are even TV shows about it. Some people are even turning it into a business, so it may be worth a dabble if you are good with your hands.

11. Thankfully, most electronic devices are rechargeable these days but if you still have to use batteries, then buy rechargeable ones. They work very well and the initial price is paid back within about three charges

12. Try not to waste food. Have a meal planning system so you don't generate waste, use shopping lists so you don't overbuy, and know the difference between 'use by date' (do your best to eat it before that date) and 'best before date' (if it smells and looks fine beyond that date, eat it). If you do end up having food waste you can put it into council food waste collection bins (cooked) or compost (uncooked – as mentioned below).

13. Compost. Some composters can take everything and are sealed against rats and other pests. Other bins are not so sealed and you have to avoid meat or cooked foods if you want to avoid pests.

14. Issue a Christmas or birthday wish list and put the things you'd like to buy on it. Your buyers will thank you because they don't have to worry about what to buy you and you'll be happy too because you get what you want (even if it is something you were going to buy anyway). Most importantly, you don't end up with presents the buyer thinks you want. Of course, if your friends and family get you everything you need and it's perfectly harmonious then there's no need to change that.

Measuring waste

As I said above, there are limited ways to put a number on waste, so here's a quick quiz to do just that. It covers both buying and dealing with waste sustainably because the issues are so interlinked. Look at the tables below and score yourself out of a total of 10 accordingly.

How many of the 14 tips above do you employ to reduce or recycle waste? (Of course, feel free to substitute tips that you do that aren't on the list.)

0 tips	1–3 tips	4–6 tips	7–8 tips	9–11 tips	12–14 tips
0 points	1 point	2 points	3 points	4 points	5 points

Which of these statements applies when you are buying?

Just buy whatever I want regardless	Rarely look at sustainability labels before choosing	Some-times look at sustainability labels before choosing	Often look at sustainability labels before choosing	Frequently look at sustainability labels before choosing	Rigorous sustainability assessment of everything I buy
0 points	1 point	2 points	3 points	4 points	5 points

Add up both sets of points for your marks out of 10.

Perhaps in the future we will be able to measure how much waste someone produces. Banks may start to estimate carbon emissions from your purchases, which would be a great way to keep an eye on these things (see Mastercard 2021). I know someone who has designed such a scheme and I expect it will be a broad brush, but it will give an easy ready reckoner for those interested.

Marketing

We're all aware of the marketing tricks that are played on us to make us buy more, whether or not those items will satisfy a need. Everything, even where items are placed on the supermarket shelves, influences our buying decisions. But what if marketing was first and foremost about satisfying our real needs? Here's an idea for an authoritative platform that can act as a promoter of wellbeing goods and services:

1. Each quarter the platform issues the latest wellbeing statistics (in Maslow format, naturally) which shows actual performance of each region and a gap analysis showing where improvements are needed. This could be similar to what we get from the Bank of England interest rates twice every quarter on the news. These rates may or may not prompt us to look at our savings and other finances. So a wellbeing report could prompt us to look at our long-term wellbeing.

2. Subscribers (free subscription) are invited to do their own long-term wellbeing assessment (in Maslow style) and have a personalised gap analysis for their own happiness.

3. With the permission of the subscriber, the platform makes introductions to local providers of goods and services that can help the subscriber close the gap, eg an introduction to a solar PV installer or a life coach. It should also link to free resources to help subscribers.

4. If the deal is made the provider of the goods or service pays a commission to the promoting platform.

5. The commission helps pay for the promotion of the platform and for the research to generate the quarterly wellbeing reports.

Crime

Crime threatens our security, so it is worth looking into crime rates where you live. There are various sites (for example, ourwatch.org. uk/crime-prevention/crime-prevention/crime-map) that allow you to look up the number and type of crimes occurring in your area but at a national level, figures for the type of crime and the number of incidents per 1,000 people in England and Wales are:

- violence against the person offences: 32
- theft offences: 23
- fraud and computer misuse: 15
- crimes against society (eg drug possession): 15
- criminal damage and arson: 8
- sexual offences: 3
- robbery offences: 1

The ONS reports growing fraud rates, so that will be something to take particular notice of.

For new homes there is an initiative called Secured by Design. It used to be a requirement of the Code for Sustainable Homes, and some sections – for example, those that cover secure doors and windows – are now included in UK building regulations. It is a good initiative that even includes layouts of new estates (one suggestion is that planting against walls can deter graffiti) as well as third party certification of locks.

Most of us don't live in homes built to those standards but there is thankfully some good advice around. Your local police force will have specific advice for the prevalent crimes in your area but the Neighbourhood Watch scheme (ourwatch.org.uk) has some great toolkits on how to prevent crimes and so too does the national police (police.uk/pu/advice-crime-prevention). Between the two websites you can look up everything, from tips to prevent assault to Hajj fraud.

Ultimately, it would be best to live in a world with no crime or terrorism. It will take a lot of work to unravel the causes of crime and what turns people to crime but I can't help feeling that a 100 per cent crime and terrorism-free world is possible. The first hurdle is to get other people to believe that. I've had many conversations with people who simply believe that crime is a part of life and that a zero-crime world is physically and biologically impossible. I can't help thinking that if everyone's wellbeing was at 100 per cent there would be no incentive to commit crime against fellow humans. There are plenty of countries with lower crime rates than us, so perhaps we can learn something from them.

Money

You've probably gleaned by now that having lots of money is not a biological necessity for a happy and fulfilling life. However, due to the way we humans have decided to organise ourselves, money is essential to acquire our basic and security needs, as well as a means to satisfy our higher wellbeing needs. So, until other systems of organising ourselves evolve we are going to have to acquire some money.

I'm not a professional financial advisor so I can only signpost you to the government's financial wellbeing strategy, which aims to have more of us financially secure by 2030 (Money & Pensions Service 2020). Perhaps that will guide you and your family on your way to financial security. I will note, though, that the strategy seems to be more about managing your money once you have it rather than how to acquire enough of it to pay for essentials. However, the strategy does state that it must be part of a wider system, so time will tell if it works.

Here are the strategic aims:

139

1. Financial foundations – teaching children about finances, including encouraging them to manage even small amounts of money.

2. Nation of savers – getting us all in the habit of saving regularly so we have a level of resilience. Interestingly, the strategy states that '71 per cent of adults receive unexpected bills every year'. It's not mentioned in the strategy, but a common rule of thumb is to have three months' worth of essential outgoings saved up in an instant-access account.

3. Credit counts – better credit management tools and cheaper credit rates.

4. Better debt advice – better products and services to prevent getting into debt in the first place and then better management if you do happen to fall into debt.

5. Future focus – making sure we all have good pensions and long-term savings and 'putting later-life financial and health choices in writing while they still have the physical and mental capacity to do so'.

There is also potential to improve environmental sustainability via our pensions. You can decide to ensure that your pension funds are invested in companies that are doing good or are making improvements. You will have to seek professional advice about this but it is possible and the impacts are colossal. My consultancy company took a look at this issue and here is what we found.

Recently a client asked us about carbon emissions associated with investments in pension schemes and whether this is something that is discussed in the social housing sector. Carbon emissions can indeed be associated with the investment of pension schemes. The classic example is when pension funds are invested in oil companies which, when their oil is combusted, results in CO_2 emissions, so how significant are these emissions and should they be included in carbon reporting for social landlords?

Pensions are some of the world's largest investments, with total private pension wealth in Great Britain at £6.1 trillion in April 2016–March 2018 (ONS 2019). While these investments are meant to support individuals in elderly life, many are also hindering our future at the same time through investing in fossil fuels. By the time many people have access to these funds, climate change may have affected food prices due to increased severity of droughts lowering crop yields. Similarly, insurance prices may have increased due to the frequency of extreme weather events and sea level rises. A recent report found that the UK pensions industry enables the release of more CO_2 than the entire footprint of the UK, and that £60 of every £1,000 invested in pension funds goes into fossil fuel companies, including giants like Shell and BP (Cooper 2021).

If relevant, companies should also account for the emissions of the investee or project, eg if a pension provider provides equity/debt financing to a window manufacturer, the financial institution is required to account for the proportional emissions from that manufacturer. CO_2 emissions data associated with each pension fund is slowly becoming more available. This will eventually help other investors to decide which pension fund to use.

How significant are these investments?

The Make My Money Matter report (2021) analysed £1.9 trillion of the £2.7 trillion in assets under management in the UK's pensions. It found that 70 per cent of leading pension schemes have failed to set robust net zero commitments building on an absence of data and poor transparency within the industry, despite growing public demand.

The report found that these pension schemes fund an estimated 330 million tonnes of carbon emissions every year, with £112 billion (6 per cent) invested in fossil fuels. This results in an estimated 176.79 kg carbon emissions per pound invested in pension funds on average.

What can you do?

Putting pressure on pension providers and increasing the demand for sustainable investments will have a big impact. Below are some suggested methods to increase the demand for ethical investments:

- ⌃ Research and find out more about where your pension investments are going.

- ⌃ Switch to ethical investment funds with your providers.

- ⌃ If you are an employer, demand more sustainable investments from your pension providers.

Scoring security

Chapters 5, 6 and 7 provided great ways to evaluate your own contribution to environmental and physical security. So how can we rate our security for the purposes of our matrix on page vii? To give yourself a security rating to put into the scoring matrix, complete this sub-matrix:

Issue	Your answer in %	Notes
Energy efficiency of your home (SAP rating)	(your SAP)/85 * 100	If you don't know, then you could use the average UK of SAP of 65 until you know more
Water security	130/your lpd from your bills * 100	If you don't know, you can use 142 lpd

Overheating resilience	If 1–2 risk factors then 100%. 3 risk factors = 75% 4 risk factors = 50% 5 risk factors = 25% 6 risk factors = 0 %	You can adjust these figures if you think you can resolve the issue, eg drop the number of risk factors if your home has external shading installed
Flood resilience	Look at the highest flood risk for your home and use these scores: High = 96 7% Medium = 97.9% Low = 99.0% Very low = 99.9%	If you've taken measures to protect yourself in any of these zones, you can upgrade your score
Air quality	Look up the DAQIs for your region for the last year and count up the number of days it's 1,2 or 3 (you might need a spreadsheet). Your air quality is then days with DAQI 1–3 last year/365 days * 100	
Wildlife garden	How many of the four RSPB tips apply to your garden? Your answer is: tip = 25% 2 tips = 50% 3 tips = 75% 4 tips = 100%	If you don't have a garden, score yourself 100% for not occupying so much land!
Green travel	Your judgement I'm afraid – 100% = walk everywhere and completely offset any travel that uses fossil fuels; 0% is you have a huge fuel guzzler and drive everywhere and take flights as much as possible!	There's really no easy way of doing this at household level but you'll have a good idea
Buying stuff and waste	Score from the quiz above and multiply by 10	

Crime security	You need to look for Crime in England and Wales: Police Force Area data tables, which will give more detail of total recorded crimes per 1,000 people in your area. The formula is [1,000 – your figure]/1,000 * 100	If you can't find the exact figure, use the national average which is 93.3% at time of writing. You can make adjustments if you think any things you have put in place increase your security
Financially secure	Your judgement again – 100% = no debt worries and have a great pension; 0% is you don't know where your next meal is coming from	
Average	Add up all the % above and divide by 10.	

You now need to convert this into marks out of 25 for the matrix on page vii. Do this by multiplying by 0.25. You'll note that this is not the exact set of questions to compare to the UK average but the things you do make an overall contribution to aspects of security like food for everyone. And provided you're consistent, you can monitor your progress towards a more secure life.

Chapter 8
Emotional and social wellbeing

The previous chapters dealt with physical things – the fabric and running of our homes and how we go about satisfying our basic and security needs. Although there is some variation, the things we need to do to improve our basic wellbeing and security are broadly the same. However, satisfying social, esteem and self-actualisation needs will vary hugely between different people. Vast amounts of research have been undertaken to try to identify which factors make people happy.

Some of this research will have a vested interest – for example, gardening magazines will say that gardening improves wellbeing and might even quantify that. For example, 'People who garden have 6.6 per cent higher wellbeing scores than those who don't.' (Rigby 2021)

Erasmus University in the Netherlands has catalogued these studies together with the statistics behind them and come up with some universal aspects of emotional and social wellbeing. An example of the type of data stored in this catalogue is about religion.

A 1990 study in Argentina found that people who answered 'yes' to the question 'Do you belong to a religious denomination?' had a happiness score of 3.09 (on a scale of 0 = not happy to 4

= very happy) compared with 2.97 for those who answered 'no' (Timmermans 1997). More recently Villani et al. (2019) found that religious people scored 4.67 on a subjective wellbeing scale compared to 4.30 for those who weren't religious.

There is lots of data in the Erasmus University database but it's not that easy to navigate to find out answers to questions such as whether or not being married or having children improves your subjective wellbeing. Plus, the statistics are really for statisticians and social researchers to navigate.

For a round-up of recent wellbeing research, a book I would recommend is *The Year of Living Danishly* by Helen Russel (2015). She finds herself in Denmark for a year and while there she speaks to various academics and other people to try and discover why Denmark so often scores highly as one of the happiest countries in the world. It's an entertaining and informative account and it was great to read it through the Maslow lens. You'll learn about dancing cows, winter swimming, egalitarian car number plates and safety nets for divorced couples.

I witnessed some egalitarian behaviour when I was in Copenhagen once. I took part in a parkrun, which had two laps. Unlike in the UK parkrun system, the second lap was in the reverse direction to the first lap. This meant that you never lapped anyone, meaning that faster runners could enjoy a fast run and slower runners never got demotivated by being lapped.

As an environmentalist I would love to be able to tell you that walking in forests or swimming in clean rivers or eating organic food is the only way to true happiness. I'm sure all those things contribute to a lot of people's wellbeing but everyone satisfies their wellbeing needs in different ways. Nevertheless, the advice coming from the research does point to improved wellbeing gained from walks in nature and experiencing the outdoors. And if you are going to boost your self-esteem in some way, why not do this by completing environmental-based study projects?

There are no definitive answers yet but there are emerging themes. So to simplify things, this chapter will contain some self-diagnostics and then some signposting of things to try. Most of the suggestions listed here come from the following authoritative sources:

- The What Works Centre for Wellbeing (whatworkswell being.org/about-wellbeing/what-affects-wellbeing) – this is a source of data cited in HM Treasury's 'Wellbeing guidance for appraisal: Supplementary Green Book guidance' (2021)

- The NHS '5 steps to mental wellbeing' (nhs.uk/mental-health/self-help/guides-tools-and-activities/five-steps-to-mental-wellbeing) – positive psychologists worked together to create this equivalent to the 'eat five a day' message.

- Mind – a mental health charity with some excellent resources.

Everything in these sources maps very easily onto a Maslow framework. Each of the sections begins with a question for you to evaluate your own score, followed by tips from the sources above. If you score highly then, in general, that's all good. However, if what you are doing is enjoyable but potentially unsustainable (eg Formula 1 racing) then it may be worth looking at ways to make your activity more sustainable. If you score particularly low then the Mind advice below will be more appropriate. If you're worried about your mental health then please seek more professional advice.

Social needs

How often have you felt lonely? The percentage of the population who answered this question respectively is given below for the UK pre-lockdown:

- often/always – 6.1 per cent
- some of the time – 16.7 per cent
- occasionally – 23.4 per cent
- hardly ever – 32.0 per cent
- never – 21.9 per cent.

What's your answer? If you answered, 'hardly ever' or 'never', then you are probably perfectly happy with the social contact you have and it'll be just a case of maintaining that level of social contact that suits you. If you answered 'often/always' then it's probably worth considering professional help or looking at Mind's advice (from mind.org.uk/information-support/tips-for-everyday-living/loneliness/tips-to-manage-loneliness):

1. Take it slowly – there is no need to rush to meet loads of new people and you can do it online to start with.
2. Make new connections – join a class or group or try volunteering.
3. Try peer support groups – see the Mind website (mind.org) for some links.
4. Try to open up – if you have lots of friends but you don't feel close to them you might try opening up to them.
5. Talking therapies – these help you explore and understand your feelings of loneliness.
6. Social care – the law places general obligations on local authorities to promote wellbeing and to prevent social care needs from arising.
7. Be careful when comparing yourself to others, for example on social media. You are only seeing one side of that person and you've no idea what their life is like when their social media feed is off.

8. Look after yourself – diet, sleep, physical activity and enjoying green spaces and animals.

If you answered 'some of the time' or 'occasionally' then the general advice might be helpful to you. Here are some of the NHS '5 steps':

- ⅄ Connect with other people – arrange days out with friends you haven't seen for a while, play a game, volunteer, or use technology to stay in touch (but don't rely on it to build relationships).

- ⅄ Give to others – say thank you for things, volunteer, help people with DIY or other projects.

- ⅄ Get physically active – why not do this with a group?

The What Works Centre for Wellbeing explains the factors that are important to our wellbeing:

- ⅄ What we do – things like working, volunteering, participating in sports (in this context with a club), being satisfied in our work (arguably work that gives us social connection as well as satisfying other needs).

- ⅄ Being able to access key services and natural environments.

- ⅄ A spiritual life or belief system – this can have the advantage of meeting other people with common belief systems.

- ⅄ A sense of belonging with our neighbourhood.

- ⅄ Having good relationships.

- ⅄ Having people you can rely on.

Work seems to feature a lot in both the What Works resources and in the Treasury guide to wellbeing assessment. Measuring how 'good' work is for people is an innovative aspect of the government's 'Building a Britain fit for the future' strategy which came out in

2017. This was perhaps the most innovative part of the strategy as it is the part that, if acted upon, has the prospect of making a big difference to wellbeing. The idea is that the government will start to measure how good work and employment are. It will then use this measure to ensure that employers provide good work and a good working environment. The idea is still very much in its infancy and is starting with conversations with unions as well as the Confederation of British Industry, which says:

> *This conversation will begin with the aspects that we believe are foundational: overall worker satisfaction; good pay; participation and progression; wellbeing, safety and security; and voice and autonomy.* (HM Government 2017)

A lot has happened since the strategy was released and it's hard to track exactly how the strategy is evolving but as we've seen, there do seem to be moves afoot to deal with wellbeing.

Social acceptance

It's not only important how often we have social interactions but also the quality of those interactions. For example, there is an ideal ratio of praise to criticism (see Flora 2000, for example), which will be useful to you as both a receiver and a giver. Many people enjoy a bit of banter but there comes a point when it gets too much if it's not balanced and it turns out that the ideal ratio is five praises to one criticism. Something to think about when you are with friends.

Esteem

If I were to ask you to mark out of 10 how worthwhile are the things you do, with 0 being not at all and 10 being completely, what would you say? Pre-pandemic, 36.1 per cent of people over 16 answered 9 or 10. If you answered 9 or 10, then keep on going, particularly if what you are doing helps other people satisfy their own needs. If you score 0 or 1, then I'd suggest that Mind's advice (see mind. org.uk/information-support/types-of-mental-health-problems/ self-esteem/tips-to-improve-your-self-esteem) or professional advice will be useful for you:

- ⚑ be kind to yourself – get to know yourself, let yourself have feelings and think about what self-esteem means for you

- ⚑ look after yourself – sleep, diet, time outside, physical activity

- ⚑ try to notice the good things – celebrate success, accept compliments, ask people what they like about you

- ⚑ build a support network – see Mind's website for good links

- ⚑ access talking and arts therapies

- ⚑ learn to be assertive – this includes learning to say 'no' and not taking too much on

- ⚑ set yourself a challenge – do things you enjoy or take up a new hobby or volunteering, set yourself small goals

- ⚑ find support for connected issues – see the website for links for people affected by abuse or bullying.

If you score between 2 and 8, then the NHS advice might again be helpful:

- ⚑ Being physically active can raise your self-esteem – one of the key benefits I found with parkrun is the reports you get on each run. There are so many data points you are bound to be good in one of the categories, eg in top 25 per cent of males over 50, or most runs done, or most volunteering shifts completed. The NHS stresses that physical activity doesn't need to mean hours in a gym but rather choosing physical activities that you enjoy.

> ⅄ Learn new skills – new recipes, new responsibilities at work (or mentoring others), signing up for a course. There's no need to do exams if that's not your thing.

The What Works website also lists being engaged in formal or informal learning as a way to develop our education and learning.

One of the things that Maslow pointed out is that, in general, we need to satisfy our needs at the lower levels before we can satisfy the higher needs such as esteem and self-actualisation, so you might start by ensuring reasonable social connection at the same time as building up your self-esteem.

Self-actualisation

This is the big one and yet it has not really been explored much in terms of putting a measurement on it. The overall life satisfaction question we asked on page 70 is possibly as good a place to start as any. There is also the question of how much leisure time you have, as you need time to pursue your peak experiences, assuming you are not gaining them from work (or volunteering – you'll notice this is a common theme in the lists above!).

So, Q1: Rate on a scale of 0 to 10 your satisfaction with life overall, where 0 is not at all and 10 is completely. (Pre-pandemic 30.7 per cent of people scored 9 or 10.)

Q2: Rate your level of satisfaction with your leisure time. The stats from 2017 recorded by the ONS (see ons.gov.uk/people populationandcommunity/wellbeing) were:

> ⅄ completely satisfied – 17.0 per cent
>
> ⅄ mostly satisfied – 27.8 per cent
>
> ⅄ somewhat satisfied – 19.5 per cent

- neither satisfied nor dissatisfied – 13.4 per cent

- somewhat dissatisfied – 12.9 per cent

- mostly dissatisfied – 6.2 per cent

- completely dissatisfied – 3.1 per cent.

You can do some further diagnostics about your own self-actualisation on various tests online. One of them is derived from Maslow's work – see scottbarrykaufman.com/selfactualizationtests.

If you score 9/10 for Q1 or completely/or mostly satisfied for Q2, then you are probably doing fine, so keep on and make sure your activities are sustainable so you can keep doing them. If Q1 is 0–1 then check your answers to the social and esteem questions and see if they shed any light on what you can do. The Mind website doesn't have specific advice for lack of self-actualisation but the only NHS '5 steps' tip left is this: 'Pay attention to the present moment (mindfulness).' So this might be something worth trying if your social and esteem ratings are very good. Here's Mind's advice on mindfulness:

- Make sure it's right for you – mindfulness is a general wellbeing tool and it works for some people and not others. If you have specific issues, then it may be better to gain specialist advice on those issues.

- Mindfulness helps you become more self-aware, feel calmer and less stressed, feel more able to choose how to respond to your thoughts and feelings, cope with difficult or unhelpful thoughts and be kinder towards yourself.

- There are various techniques and they involve paying close attention to your body during various activities. I particularly like the tips on practising mindfulness in nature – another good reason to protect our environment.

Another way to travel

One of the ways many people attain self-actualisation is through travel – and travel is heavily marketed. I talked about transport as part of our basic and security needs in Chapter 7. However, unlike satisfying our basic and security needs, travel to satisfy our social, esteem and self-actualisation needs is not a biological absolute, which means it's an optional thing to do. We might all feel the need for a holiday but could it be that we are really feeling the need to satisfy other biological needs that travel provides? If so, we might be able to satisfy those same needs in different ways? I'm not going to be a spoilsport and say you should never travel but plenty of people are quite happy staying local. And of course, during the pandemic, lots of us were forced to do this. Hopefully we were pleasantly surprised by what our local area can offer and how ingenious we can be. I know one family who pitched a tent in their garden to simulate a camping trip. And I heard of another couple who slept in a different bedroom in their house, just to create the idea of change.

There is a plan to combat aeroplane emissions by 2050, mainly via offsetting and developing different low-carbon fuels. There are also plans to create electric aeroplanes, which can be recharged with renewable energy. Norway's internal flight fleet has committed to going 100 per cent electric by 2040, and several individuals have created and travelled in electric planes. Some of these planes are fascinating. For example, there are designs for electric planes that will have lots of propellers on the front of the wings. On the plane's descent, the air rushing past the propeller blades will turn them and generate electricity to charge the battery. DHL have already bought electric planes for some of their deliveries. But that's all for the future. Here are some official emissions from different types of transport that we may use for leisure travel, including a reminder from Chapter 7:

- ▲ national rail: 0.03549 kg CO_2e per passenger km travelled
- ▲ international rail travel: 0.00446 kg CO_2e per passenger km travelled
- ▲ sea ferry, average passenger: 0.112862 kg CO_2e per passenger km travelled
- ▲ international air travel to European countries: 0.15353 kg CO_2e per passenger km travelled (more for business class travel); this figure includes other climate change effects from water vapour, contrails and NOx.

It's no surprise to see that plane flight is the worst. So what's a sustainable form of travel for leisure? In the future let's hope that plane flights do become net zero. Until then here are some tips.

Try swapping flying for other forms of travel – you can get surprisingly far on international trains and railway stations are typically easier to navigate than airports. For places like the Mediterranean there's no doubt it will take longer to get there, but what a nice trip it would be with various stopovers en route. There is also an incentive to travel more lightly because you don't want to carry too many bags on the train. To combat the extra time for very long distances, wouldn't it be great if the production of all our basic needs was so efficient that we didn't need to work so much and could have much longer holidays? Then there'd be less pressure to get to our destination as quickly as possible. Is that a 'flight' of fancy? I'll explore why it might not be as far fetched as you think in Chapter 9.

I've taken the train to go skiing in the Alps, hiking in northern Spain, attend a party in the Netherlands and, like a lot of people, to visit Paris. It's a great way to travel and very easy to book. You can also get some good deals, especially during school holidays. Parents will have noticed how holiday travel increases during school holidays but train prices don't and with a bit of planning you really can get some excellent deals. My rule of thumb is to book the train tickets about 12 weeks in advance (not earlier). This is when the cheap tickets are typically issued.

easyJet has a policy of not flying between any two destinations that can be reached within four hours by train. I think this is a pretty good barometer. If we're serious about our environmental credentials, we must vote with our feet. I recall once meeting a potential client for environmental work in Manchester. I had travelled from London by train, which is an extremely easy trip. I eventually won the work and, according to the people I was visiting, one of the deciding factors was that one of the competitors had flown from London to Manchester.

If you feel you need to fly and you feel guilty about it, then you can try offsetting. Offsetting is where you pay some money to an organisation that will do a carbon reduction project elsewhere. The most common offsetting is to plant trees somewhere else, the idea being that the carbon saved from that project will equal the carbon you caused by flying. It all sounds good, but offsetting is fraught with difficulties. The government's guidance on offsetting gives a steer (HM Government 2019):

- ⌃ additionality – projects must demonstrate that they have produced a saving in carbon that would not have happened otherwise

- ⌃ avoiding leakage – projects must demonstrate that they have not caused an increase in carbon emissions elsewhere

- ⌃ permanence – forestry projects are at risk of disease or fire

- ⌃ validation and verification – projects must receive independent verification

- ⌃ timing – carbon credits must only have been issued from the project after the emissions reduction has taken place

- ⌃ avoiding double counting – a registry must be used to

register, track and permanently cancel credits to avoid double counting or double selling

⋏ transparency – credits should be supported by publicly available information on a registry to set out the underlying projects, the quantification methodology applied, independent validation and verification procedures, project documentation, proof of credit ownership and date of retirement of credits.

On top of all that, what is the price of a tonne of carbon? If as an individual you wanted to buy an offset, you might pay around £6 per tonne from a website. But the European Trading Scheme is around £80 per tonne. And the UK government has a Treasury guide to 'convert' carbon savings into a £ value so they can evaluate new policies. Their central price is £241 per tonne of CO_2e and by 2050 their highest price is expected to be £568 per tonne (BEIS 2021).

One thing I've done in the past is use a hybrid offset system. I used an online calculator (clevel.co.uk/flight-carbon-calculator and there are many others) to calculate the emissions, then found a site that would give me a price to offset those emissions. I then donated that money to a charity that helps people in need. It's not perfect but it does make you think and you will be doing a little good. So a flight to Vienna for two of us emits 0.82 tonnes of CO_2e and to offset that costs £11.71, which I round up to £20 to a charity.

Then of course there are always staycations in the UK, although for a lot of people I know having sunshine is really important to them. I like the idea that some holiday parks such as Center Parcs have of having a big sun dome in the middle. Maybe in the future more holiday simulations will emerge. For example, China has created a fake 'Paris' and people in the UK are familiar with snow domes. One friend stated that after a few hours she felt that she had had her ski 'fix' for the year.

Sometimes the only thing that will change the idea of the traditional holiday is a mindset shift. Here's an account of something we did, even before the pandemic.

How we went around the world and saved 6 tonnes of carbon

For various reasons, including our carbon footprint, one year we decided on a staycation. The accommodation was our own home and no long car journeys or plane rides were involved. We 'visited' five countries and had a couple of 'resort days' where we simply relaxed and mooched about locally. We experienced international cuisine and a range of activities and had a lovely time. Our accommodation was first class, as was the service: we knew what to expect and we got it. Overall it was a winner and some of our friends have been inspired to do it too. We live in Stroud, Gloucestershire, so we looked to our local area for inspiration. Here's what we did (for the emissions figures, we used an online calculator for two people flying between London and the capital city of each country).

Greek day – Water sports by the 'sea' (1.5 tonnes saved)

After a breakfast of yoghurt, nuts, seeds, honey and fruit we headed off to Cotswold Water Park to enjoy water sports and a picnic 'at the seaside'. We tried windsurfing, paddleboarding and swimming followed by a lovely Greek salad bursting with juicy tomatoes, olives and feta cheese. In the evening we dined out at a great Greek restaurant at Gloucester Quays, where we started our evening with ouzo cocktails by the water.

Spanish day – a walk and a tour of a 'Spanish' vineyard (0.78 tonnes saved)

We started the day by making homemade churros and chocolate sauce, which was fun, delicious and set up us nicely for a relaxing morning reading in our sunny garden. Lunch was fajitas eaten al fresco (possibly Mexican instead of Spanish!) followed by a stunning two-and-a-half hour walk across the Cotswold Way to Woodchester Vineyard, where we had a lovely and informative time followed by a taxi ride home where a film and sangria awaited us.

Tyrol day – walking in the 'Alps' (0.78 tonnes saved)

The highest part of the Cotswold Way is particularly craggy so that served as the Alps. We'd had a breakfast of salad, cheese and yoghurt and were soon ready for our picnic with fantastic views. The huge cows we saw completed the landscape for us.

Canadian day – paddling a Canadian canoe (3.22 tonnes saved)

It had to be crispy bacon, maple syrup and pancakes for breakfast before we set off nice and early to Ross-on-Wye to paddle a Canadian canoe. We'd already had to rearrange this day due to the river being swollen and unsafe after huge downpours of rain (climate change?). We stopped on the way in the Forest of Dean in the hope of seeing beavers in a trial they are running there. I'm pretty sure I saw the back end of one! We enjoyed a sunny afternoon canoeing and saw kingfishers and an egret. We're told that chips, cheese and gravy is really quite Canadian and we enjoyed it at home in the evening.

English Cotswolds Day – Stroud farmers' market and local walk (0 tonnes used nor saved)

Stroud farmers' market is an award-winning market that takes place every Saturday and as it is right on our doorstep this had to be one of our destinations. We had our breakfast there and bought lots of goodies, including goats' cheese, gin, chorizo, local honey and hot tomato salsa for our walk and picnic later on that day.

So there you have it: lots of experiences from around the world right on our doorstep and still a great holiday. Plus, a 'tongue in cheek' 6 tonnes of carbon saved.

Big houses and fast cars

As with travel, there seems to be a desire for some people to have big houses, fast cars, the latest gadgets, the fanciest foods. We know that shelter, food and getting around are essential for our needs but how does having a huge house fit into the Maslow framework? Does it make us happy? I suspect that these extravagant things are in fact satisfying other needs like social acceptance, esteem and maybe even a bit of self-actualisation. Maybe interior decorating projects are your thing but you can still make them sustainable. Why not have a huge house that is net zero? Why not have a fast car that is electric and charged off a solar array? Why not have fancy foods and clothes but ensure they are sustainably sourced as best you can?

Of course, an alternative to owning a car is just to use one when you need it. Let's face it, most of the time that hunk of metal is just sitting there doing nothing. If we could move to sharing one car between many people this would cut down on the environmental impacts of producing many cars for each person. It's likely that this option is more viable for occasional, higher Maslow level uses than securing our basic needs, which is why I've included this suggestion here.

You could investigate moving to some kind of car sharing arrangement. The most obvious is a car share club but an alternative is to hire a car when you need it – say to drive on a week's holiday somewhere. The advantage is that you get a reasonable car and, depending on how many times you use it, it could work out cheaper than owning a car. This way, the car hire process simply becomes part of the holiday planning.

You've seen how your wellbeing needs are inextricably linked to your impact on the planet. You've measured how you can improve your happiness and security by rethinking how you live both at home and elsewhere. You might have found some or all of the ideas useful on a personal level or even on an organisational level if you run a business or social enterprise. But what if you could combine this knowledge and really change how our society operates from the bottom up? What if we could change things on a larger scale? Is it really impossible to create 100 per cent happiness for 100 per cent of the people 100 per cent of the time?

Chapter 9
Other worlds are possible

We have all grown up in and live in a world where money seems to be the be-all and end-all – the measure of success. What's more, we live in a monetary system that is designed for and rigged towards wealthy people acquiring more wealth (see Monbiot 2016 for a good overview of the neoliberalism world view behind this). It isn't designed for the benefit of us all. That's not to say wealth hasn't brought benefits (it has made food and shelter more affordable, for example) but it is certainly not the panacea for all human wellbeing. The current system has led to inequality, divided societies and other social ills. The mantra 'the market will provide' certainly didn't prevent the Covid-19 pandemic, even though there were plenty of warnings of such an outbreak prior to the event.

It's easy to feel that this is the world as it is and nothing can change that. But in this chapter, I want to show you that, in fact, other worlds (non-money based) have existed before us and other future worlds (probably non-money based) are possible. But we have to work towards creating that world. What's more, we have to believe that that world really is possible.

If you happen to be in a position of authority in an organisation, or even if you aspire to be that person (which may well satisfy some of your needs), this section provides tools to make those important first steps to a world where everyone has all their human needs satisfied: a world where everyone has plenty of food, water, shelter and clean air; a world free from conflict and designed to maximise physical and mental health. In other words, 100 per cent wellbeing for 100 per cent of the people.

Life version 3.0

In the book *Life 3.0*, Swedish-American cosmologist Max Tegmark (2017) explains machine learning and explores different worlds in which artificial intelligence and robots play a predominant role. Of course, some scary stories appear where humans are essentially redundant and the robots take over – quite the stuff of science fiction and dystopian future films. But could this become a reality? People are already worried about their jobs being replaced by robots and computers. Many types of manual work have already been replaced, and legal and medical work are also increasingly being automated. One of the proposed responses to this is the concept of universal basic income, where everyone gets a wage that pays for their basic needs. That way, it won't matter that robots have taken over their jobs.

I have a military friend who told me about an oil-rich country where their government does exactly that. Each family is paid a salary and they don't have to do anything for it. However, there still seems to be discontent in that country, which may mean that other needs are not being met. Is this universal payment a sort of social contract where people get paid for not upsetting the government?

Of course, other versions of this could emerge in the future. We could have a world in which automation and robots take care of our basic needs such as food (there is already lots going on to automate agriculture), shelter (take a look on YouTube for videos of 3D-printed houses) and making sure that our supplies of water and air are kept clean. Automation could also take care of high-quality hospitals, schools and possibly some form of security service that ensures we don't slip back into the old world. After that it remains for us to be social, maximise our self-esteem and self-actualise, none of which needs to cost money or the world's resources. Moving from a maximum-money world to a no-money world would take some doing, as our mindset is currently fixated on wealth. But if you think about it hard it is the most natural thing in the world, so it is always possible.

The key is to ensure that the automations are programmed to maximise our wellbeing. A hot topic in the world of artificial intelligence is how to build in a set of ethics into the automations. What would those ethics be? Getting them right would be paramount because otherwise unintended consequences could occur. For example, if you programme for zero carbon emissions, the automations might simply see that the solution is to wipe out humans who dig up and use fossil fuels. Clearly this isn't what we want for our future.

So how about we use Maslow's framework as a set of ethics for the programmers to use?

Another projection of what humans may evolve into comes from Yuval Noah Harari's book *Sapiens* (2015). In it, Harari describes previous versions of humans and how we have transitioned from hunter-gatherers to agriculturalists and all the other ages up until now. He proposes that these stages have evolved purely because of our biology. His projection for the future is that we will eventually evolve into some kind of hybrid robot species. This comes from two directions. The first is that we are already augmenting ourselves with things like heart pacemakers, tooth fillings and artificial limbs. The second is that robots are being augmented to become more and more human, with human devices like skin and bones.

Not only are other worlds possible but our actions can move us towards those worlds. Those actions can be individual actions as described in the bulk of this book, or they can be more collective actions if you happen to be in a position of authority. Here are some actions you could take to move towards a different world.

Be the boss

Hopefully your organisation already has an environmental policy. Maybe you have a wellbeing policy too but the ones I've seen seem to focus on 'absence of illness' rather than maximising wellbeing of staff and customers. If not, then here are some business case ideas to help convince senior stakeholders to adopt environmental and wellbeing policies.

- Increased sales – there is a huge growth in people wanting to buy ethical products. Firms such as Unilever and IKEA report extra sales in their ethical brands. For my own business, I have examined my marketing data and found that messages associated with wellbeing attract higher traction than the same message with a non-wellbeing title.

- Investment – the world banking industry is going through a transformation where it wants to invest in organisations that provide so-called ESG benefits. ESG stands for environment, social and governance. The investors want to see meaningful metrics on each of these issues, both in new ventures and also when refinancing existing loans, so there is big money at stake.

- Staff recruitment and retention – there is growing evidence that people want to work with and for companies with a demonstrable ethical ethos. This is true particularly of younger people who have an invested interest in the future. Easier recruitment and greater staff retention can be translated into pounds and pence to help make a business case.

- Higher productivity – people with higher levels of wellbeing are generally more productive and take fewer sick days. If the workforce has also had its self-esteem boosted by gaining extra qualifications, this adds to your arsenal of skills you can offer clients.

⋏ Operational savings – the obvious one is saving energy costs, but there are many more that aren't so obvious. Here are a few I've come across in my work:

> ✧ Housing associations have lower maintenance costs for homes that are energy efficient.
>
> ✧ Saving on flood risk insurance premiums – when a client examined what they were paying for, they found they were insuring a lot of car parks that they didn't need to cover against flooding. Removing these from the property insured resulted in a reduction in premiums.
>
> ✧ Tracker systems on vehicle fleets allow easy monitoring of carbon emissions but they also show where each vehicle is at any time, allowing for easier tracking of productivity.
>
> ✧ Strategic thinking – when the whole organisation works to a single aim there is less likelihood of one department taking action that costs another department more money.

⋏ Regulatory compliance – there are more environmental regulations emerging all the time, so being able to comply avoids fines or other sanctions.

⋏ Regulatory anticipation – by focusing on the science and the biology of humans it is easier to anticipate future regulation. This means it will be easier to reorganise your business accordingly at your own pace, rather than having to do it all of a sudden with huge associated implementation costs.

Maslow obsession

I confess that I am a bit obsessed with Maslow (I've even developed a Maslow-related board game) and part of this obsession has filtered into the way I run my environmental consultancy business. I find that using Maslow as a framework creates order and purpose to what we do. Here are some of the ways I have incorporated it into our business.

Our document filing system (which is entirely paperless) is split into our different needs. For our business this means:

- ⅄ Basic needs – this is the lifeblood of our company and consists of any files related to ongoing projects for paying clients. Included in each project file are all contractual agreements.

- ⅄ Security needs – this is everything that supports the business and ensures its long-term wellbeing, including sales proposals, certifications, insurance details, finances, our own environmental reporting, etc. On the proposals folder, once we win a client, we move the whole proposal folder into their project folder in the basic needs section. This helps keep the proposals folder tidy and not full of redundant documents.

- ⅄ Social needs – this contains the details of staff socials.

- ⅄ Esteem and self-actualisation needs – these are dealt with by individuals themselves.

The second way Maslow has influenced our business processes is as a framework for our monthly one-to-one and team meetings. These are split into:

- ⅄ Basic needs – at one-to-one level we drill down on any technical issues on live projects and at team level we have progress updates on live projects.

⌃ Security needs – at team meetings I show the team the number of leads we have in the pipeline. We also organise annual environmental reporting and quality assurance items, etc that keep the business going for the long term.

⌃ Social needs – these are the details of staff socials so we all turn up at the right place at the right time!

⌃ Esteem needs – one-to-one level only. This is where we get to discuss training, professional qualifications or other self-development opportunities that overlap with our business aims. Like any business there is always a risk that you will spend time training people up only for them to leave but I like a quote that's been attributed to Richard Branson: 'Train people so they are good enough to leave but treat them so that they don't want to.'

⌃ Self-actualisation needs – this is an opportunity to see if there are any other issues and that work/life balance is OK.

Our quality system is geared towards helping our clients make environmental improvements. This is a subtle but specific difference to the usual client satisfaction surveys. At the end of each contract one of the questions we ask is 'On a scale of 0–10, how much has and/or will the project completed with SHIFT Environment contribute towards environmental improvements in your organisation? (0 being no influence and 10 being fundamental to the improvements).' I'm pleased to say that at the time of writing, the average feedback is 8.6 out of 10.

Cut out and keep wellbeing strategy

A while back a friend asked me to draft a wellbeing strategy that they could suggest to their company. You might find it useful too, so here it is:

Suggestion summary

My suggestion is for the company to take a strategic approach to employee wellbeing. The strategy should include a key performance indicator (KPI) for measuring wellbeing, an objective of maximising wellbeing for all employees and regular reporting of progress.

Benefits for the company

Improved employee wellbeing will:

- improve productivity by getting projects completed on time and to budget
- improve staff retention by reducing recruitment costs
- align with UK (and other) government strategies to increase chances of gaining more contracts with these clients.

Suggestions for a wellbeing KPI

The government's most recent industrial strategy states that they intend to measure 'good work'. It will explore: overall worker satisfaction; good pay; participation and progression; wellbeing, safety and security; and voice and autonomy. The Office of National Statistics (ONS) has also been measuring wellbeing for a number of years.

In addition, Maslow's motivational theory has been proven to correlate well with overall satisfaction. Therefore I suggest that the company use Maslow's hierarchy of needs as a basis for a wellbeing KPI. This will allow an immediate gap analysis of overall employee wellbeing which will, in turn, show which actions need to be taken to improve. The KPI can be calculated using a combination of existing business data and quarterly employee mini surveys. Below is a suggestion of how this could work:

Maslow hierarchy level	Measure (%)	Possible interventions
Basic	% employees above minimum living wage	Competitive salaries
Security	• H&S data converted to % employee safety • Financial security – pensions, advice given for savings – convert to % financially secure • Environmental data* - % closeness to science-based environmental targets • Physical security – % secure from physical attack – ONS crime data	• H&S strategy • Free financial advice • Reduce environmental impacts • Liaise with local authorities in areas with high crime
Social	ONS-style question in staff mini surveys – eg marks out of 100, how satisfied are you with your social life?	• Improve work-based social networks and occasions • Encourage/allow time for external social contact visiting family and friends

Esteem	ONS-style question in staff mini-survey – eg marks out of 100, how worthwhile are the things you do?	• Encourage/support staff to gain professional recognition of their choice – eg chartered environmentalist • Match work to individuals' long-term aims • Encourage staff to enter/ win internal and/or external competitions • Encourage more qualifications • Recognise staff that contribute most to company's wellbeing objectives
Self-ac-tualisa-tion	ONS-style questions in staff mini-survey, eg marks out of 100, how satisfied are you with your work/life balance?	• Encourage good work/life balance • Ensure work aims match employee's chosen interests
Overall wellbeing	Weighted average of the above percentages	Wellbeing action plan

Using this KPI the company will see where anything falls below 100 per cent – ie where intervention is most needed.

* Environmental protection is included because things like clean air, reduced carbon emissions, flood protection, etc all contribute to the security of our basic needs.

Further implications

After a few years of monitoring and surveying each quarter, sufficient data should be available to see which interventions result in the best wellbeing outcomes. You could even convert the company's financial information into a '% business financial security' figure. Staff retention should improve and wellbeing measuring and strategy could be extended to the benefits that the company brings to clients.

Conclusion

You should now have completed the matrix on page vii for yourself and possibly for the company you run. How did you score? What is your level of wellbeing? You might not have thought about how your own happiness is linked to protecting the environment before but I hope you can now see how we cannot achieve 100 per cent happiness on a basic, security or social/esteem level without thinking about our impacts on the world around us. Neither can we expect to reach that pinnacle of wellbeing: self-actualisation. This is because satisfying our highest needs will always be inextricably linked to our significance in the world – in other words, how worthwhile we feel. If our actions fail to consider the wellbeing of those around us and the planet on which we live, we will never feel as if our existence here has been worth something.

Understanding how to measure wellbeing helps us to learn how to manage it and I hope this book has shown that there are many small – and big – changes you can make that will directly affect your happiness. From reducing your vulnerability to flooding or overheating to getting creative with your holidays and your waste, there is a world where you can control how happy you become. And if we all take steps to protect our personal wellbeing and that of the planet, we can edge towards a different world entirely.

References

Bank of England (2019) 'What is GDP?'. URL: bankofengland.co.uk/
    knowledgebank/what-is-gdp

Bank of England (2020) 'What is money?'. URL: bankofengland.co.uk/
    knowledgebank/what-is-money

BEIS (2016) 'Annual fuel poverty statistics report: 2016'. URL: gov.uk/
    government/statistics/annual-fuel-poverty-statistics-report-2016

BEIS (2021) 'Valuation of greenhouse gas emissions: for policy
    appraisal and evaluation'. URL: gov.uk/government/publications/
    valuing-greenhouse-gas-emissions-in-policy-appraisal/valuation-
    of-greenhouse-gas-emissions-for-policy-appraisal-and-evaluation

BRE (2012) 'The government's Standard Assessment Procedure for
    energy rating of dwellings'. URL: bre.co.uk/filelibrary/SAP/2012/
    SAP-2012_9-92.pdf

Committee on Climate Change (2020) 'The Sixth Carbon Budget: The UK's
    path to net zero'. URL: theccc.org.uk/wp-content/uploads/2020/12/
    The-Sixth-Carbon-Budget-The-Uks-path-to-Net-Zero.pdf

Cooper, R. (2021) 'New report finds pension funds enable more CO2 than
    the entire UK carbon footprint'. URL: climateaction.org/news/new-report-
    finds-pension-funds-enable-more-co2-than-the-entire-uk-carbon-fo

Cycling UK (2022) 'Guide e-cycle batteries'. URL: cyclinguk.org/article/guide-
    e-bike-batteries

DEFRA (2014) Food Statistics Pocketbook 2014. URL: assets.publishing.
    service.gov.uk/government/uploads/system/uploads/attachment_data/
    file/423616/foodpocketbook-2014report-23apr15.pdf

DEFRA (2021) 'Greenhouse gas reporting: conversion factors 2021'. URL:
    gov.uk/government/publications/greenhouse-gas-reporting-
    conversion-factors-2021

Department for Transport (2021) 'Decarbonising transport: A better,

greener Britain'. URL: assets.publishing.service.gov.uk/government/
uploads/system/uploads/attachment_data/file/1009448/
decarbonising-transport-a-better-greener-britain.pdf

Dfarhud, D., Malmir, M. & Khanahmadi, M. (2014). 'Happiness and health:
The biological factors – systematic review article'. *Iranian Journal of
Public Health* 43(11).

Di Domenico, S. & Fournier, M.A. (2017) 'Esteem needs'. *Encyclopedia of
Personality and Individual Differences*. URL: link.springer.com/
referenceworkentry/10.1007%2F978-3-319-28099-8_1465-1

Diamond, J. (2005) *Collapse: How societies choose to fail or survive.*
Penguin.

DLUHC (2010) 'Code for sustainable homes'. URL: assets.publishing.service.
gov.uk/government/uploads/system/uploads/attachment_data/file/5976/
code_for_sustainable_homes_techguide.pdf

DLUHC (2020) 'The charter for social housing residents: social housing
white paper'. URL: gov.uk/government/publications/the-charter-for-
social-housing-residents-social-housing-white-paper

Dunbar, R. (2010) *How Many Friends Does One Person Need? Dunbar's
number and other evolutionary quirks.* Harvard University Press.

Easterlin, R.A. (1974). 'Does economic growth improve the human lot?
Some empirical evidence.' In David, P.A. & Reder, M.W., eds, *Nations and
Households in Economic Growth: Essays in honor of Moses Abramovitz.*
Academic Press.

Ethical Consumer (2021) 'Ethical Consumer markets report 2021'. URL:
ethicalconsumer.org/research-hub/uk-ethical-consumer-markets-report

FAWC (2009) 'Farm Animal Welfare in Great Britain: Past, present and
future'. Farm Animal Welfare Council. URL: assets.publishing.service.gov.
uk/government/uploads/system/uploads/attachment_data/file/319292/
Farm_Animal_Welfare_in_Great_Britain_-_Past__Present_and_Future.
pdf

Flora, S.R. (2000) 'Praise's magic reinforcement ratio: five to one gets the job
done'. *Behavior Analyst Today* 22 September 2000. URL: thefreelibrary.
com/Praise%27s+magic+reinforcement+ratio%3A+five+to+one+gets+
the+job+done.-a0170112823

Foresight Mental Capital and Wellbeing Project (2008). 'Final Project report
– Executive summary'. The Government Office for Science. URL: gov.uk/
government/publications/mental-capital-and-wellbeing-making-the-
most-of-ourselves-in-the-21st-century

Gaynor, T. (2020) 'Climate change is the defining crisis of our time and it particularly impacts the displaced'. URL: unhcr.org/uk/news/latest/2020/11/5fbf73384/climate-change-defining-crisis-time-particularly-impacts-displaced.html

GCF (2020) 'Social value model quick reference table'. Government Commercial Function. URL: assets.publishing.service.gov.uk/government/uploads/system/uploads/attachment_data/file/940828/Social-Value-Model-Quick-Reference-Table-Edn-1.1-3-Dec-20.pdf

Harari, Y.N. (2015) *Sapiens: A brief history of humankind*. HarperCollins.

HM Government (2017) *Industrial Strategy: Building a Britain fit for the future*. URL: assets.publishing.service.gov.uk/government/uploads/system/uploads/attachment_data/file/664563/industrial-strategy-white-paper-web-ready-version.pdf

HM Government (2018) 'UK biological security strategy'. URL: assets.publishing.service.gov.uk/government/uploads/system/uploads/attachment_data/file/730213/2018_UK_Biological_Security_Strategy.pdf

HM Government (2019) *Environmental Reporting Guidelines*. URL: assets.publishing.service.gov.uk/government/uploads/system/uploads/attachment_data/file/850130/Env-reporting-guidance_inc_SECR_31March.pdf

HM Treasury (2021) 'Wellbeing guidance for appraisal: supplementary Green Book guidance'. URL: assets.publishing.service.gov.uk/government/uploads/system/uploads/attachment_data/file/1005388/Wellbeing_guidance_for_appraisal_-_supplementary_Green_Book_guidance.pdf

Housing Ombudsman Service (2021) 'Spotlight on damp and mould'. housing-ombudsman.org.uk/wp-content/uploads/2021/10/Spotlight-report-Damp-and-mould-final.pdf

IPCC (2021) 'Climate change 2021: The physical science basis'. URL: ipcc.ch/report/ar6/wg1/

Layard, R. (2005) *Happiness: Lessons from a new science*. Penguin.

Layard, R. & Oparina, E. (2021) 'Living long and living well: The WELLBY approach'. *World Happiness Report*. URL: worldhappiness.report/ed/2021/living-long-and-living-well-the-wellby-approach/

Lee, D.M., Vanhoutte, B. et al. (2016) 'Sexual health and positive subjective wellbeing in partnered older men and women'. *Journals of Gerontology B: Psychological Sciences and Social Sciences* 71(4).

London Climate Change Partnership (2013) 'Your social housing in a changing climate'. URL: climatelondon.org/wp-content/uploads/2017/11/

Your-social-housing-in-a-changing-climate.pdf

Lupo, R. (2020) 'A measure of net well-being that incorporates the effect of housing environmental impacts'. Designing Buildings. URL: designingbuildings.co.uk/wiki/A_measure_of_net_well-being_that_incorporates_the_effect_of_housing_environmental_impacts

Make My Money Matter (2021) 'UK pension industry carbon emissions analysis: October 2021'. URL: makemymoneymatter.co.uk/wp-content/uploads/2021/10/UK-Pension-Industry-Carbon-Emissions-Analysis.pdf

Maslow, A.H. (1943) 'A theory of human motivation'. *Psychological Review* 50.

Maslow, A.H. (1962) *Toward a Psychology of Being*. Wilder Publications.

Mastercard (2021) 'Mastercard unveils new carbon calculator tool for banks globally, as consumer passion for the environment grows'. URL: mastercard.com/news/press/2021/april/mastercard-unveils-new-carbon-calculator-tool

Met Office (2018) 'UKCP18 Factsheet: Sea level rise and storm surge'. URL: metoffice.gov.uk/binaries/content/assets/metofficegovuk/pdf/research/ukcp/ukcp18-fact-sheet-sea-level-rise-and-storm-surge.pdf

Monbiot, G. (2016) 'Neoliberalism – the ideology at the root of all our problems'. *The Guardian* 15 April 2016. URL: theguardian.com/books/2016/apr/15/neoliberalism-ideology-problem-george-monbiot

Money & Pensions Service (2020) 'The UK strategy for financial wellbeing'. URL: maps.org.uk/wp-content/uploads/2020/01/UK-Strategy-for-Financial-Wellbeing-2020-2030-Money-and-Pensions-Service.pdf

OECD (2013) 'Measuring well-being for development'. Conference paper, 4-5 April 2013. URL: oecd.org/site/oecdgfd/Session%203.1%20-%20GFD%20Background%20Paper.pdf

OECD (2020) 'How's Life? 2020: Measuring well-being'. URL: oecd-ilibrary.org/sites/9870c393-en/index.html?itemId=/content/publication/9870c393-en

ONS (2017) 'CSEW victimisation, confidence in police and fear of crime in England and Wales by demographic characteristics, combined years ending March 2014 to March 2016'. URL: ons.gov.uk/peoplepopulationandcommunity/crimeandjustice/adhocs/007578csewvictimisationconfidenceinpoliceandfearofcrimein englandandwalesbydemographiccharacteristicscombinedyearsending march2014tomarch2016

ONS (2019) 'Pension wealth in Great Britain: April 2016 to March 2018'. URL: ons.gov.uk/peoplepopulationandcommunity/personalandhouse

holdfinances/incomeandwealth/bulletins/pensionwealthingreatbritain/
april2016tomarch2018

ONS (2020) 'Excess winter mortality in England and Wales: 2019 to 2020
(provisional) and 2018 to 2019 (final)'. URL: ons.gov.uk/people
populationandcommunity/birthsdeathsandmarriages/deaths/bulletins/
excesswintermortalityinenglandandwales/2019to2020provisional
and2018to2019final

ONS (2021a) 'Employee workplace pensions in the UK: 2020 provisional
and 2019 final results'. URL: ons.gov.uk/employmentandlabourmarket/
peopleinwork/workplacepensions/bulletins/annualsurveyofhoursand
earningspensiontables/2020provisionaland2019finalresults

ONS (2021b) 'Crime in England and Wales: year ending June 2021'. URL:
ons.gov.uk/peoplepopulationandcommunity/crimeandjustice/bulletins/
crimeinenglandandwales/yearendingjune2021

ONS (2021c) 'Loneliness rates and well-being indicators by local authority'.
URL: ons.gov.uk/peoplepopulationandcommunity/wellbeing/datasets/
lonelinessratesandwellbeingindicatorsbylocalauthority

ONS (2021d) 'Personal well-being in the UK, quarterly: April 2011 to
September 2020'. URL: ons.gov.uk/peoplepopulationandcommunity/
wellbeing/bulletins/personalwellbeingintheukquarterly/april2011to
september2020

ONS (2022a) 'Household debt: wealth in Great Britain'. URL: ons.gov.uk/
peoplepopulationandcommunity/personalandhouseholdfinances/inco-
meandwealth/datasets/householddebtwealthingreatbritain

ONS (2022b) 'Crime in England and Wales: Appendix tables'. URL: ons.gov.
uk/peoplepopulationandcommunity/crimeandjustice/datasets/crimein
englandandwalesappendixtables

ONS (2022c) 'Consumer trends: current price, not seasonally adjusted'.
URL: ons.gov.uk/economy/nationalaccounts/satelliteaccounts/datasets/
consumertrendscurrentpricenotseasonallyadjusted

Pandemic Preparedness Partnership (2021) '100 Days Mission to respond
to future pandemic threats'. URL: gov.uk/government/publications/100-
days-mission-to-respond-to-future-pandemic-threats

Perez, I. (2013) 'Climate change and rising food prices heightened Arab
Spring'. Scientific American 4 March 2013. URL: scientificamerican.com/
article/climate-change-and-rising-food-prices-heightened-arab-spring/

Public Health England (2019) 'Public Health England publishes air pollution
evidence review'. URL: gov.uk/government/news/public-health-england-
publishes-air-pollution-evidence-review

Public Health England (2020) 'Heatwave mortality monitoring report: 2020'. URL: gov.uk/government/publications/phe-heatwave-mortality-monitoring/heatwave-mortality-monitoring-report-2020

RAC (2019) 'Tyre labels explained: fuel economy, grip and noise ratings'. URL: rac.co.uk/drive/advice/tyres/what-do-your-tyre-labels-mean/

Riahi, K., van Vuuren, D.P. et al. (2017) 'The Shared Socioeconomic Pathways and their energy, land use, and greenhouse gas emissions implications: An overview'. *Global Environmental Change* 42, January 2017. URL: sciencedirect.com/science/article/pii/S0959378016300681

Rigby, S. (2021) 'Gardening just twice a week improves wellbeing and relieves stress'. *BBC Science Focus*. URL: sciencefocus.com/news/gardening-just-twice-a-week-improves-wellbeing-and-relieves-stress

Robins, R.W, Hendin H.M. & Trzesniewski, K.H. (2001) 'Measuring global self-esteem: Construct validation of a single-item measure and the Rosenberg self-esteem scale'. *Society for Personality and Social Psychology* 27(2).

Russell, H. (2015) *The Year of Living Danishly*. Icon Books.

Shadbolt, P. (2015) 'Rumble in the jungle: can wild animals help us predict earthquakes?' CNN 3 April 2015. URL: edition.cnn.com/2015/04/03/tech/mci-earthquake-animals/

SHIFT (2021) 'IPCC climate warning – what next?'. URL: shiftenvironment.co.uk/news/ipcc-climate-warning-what-next/

State of Nature Partnership (2019) 'State of Nature: A summary for the UK'. URL: nbn.org.uk/wp-content/uploads/2019/09/State-of-Nature-2019-UK-summary.pdf

Tay L. & Diener, E. (2011) 'Needs and subjective wellbeing around the world'. *Journal of Personality and Social Psychology* 101(2).

Tegmark, M. (2017) *Life 3.0: Being human in the age of artificial intelligence.* Allen Lane.

The Environment Agency (2009) 'Water for people and the environment: Water Resources Strategy for England and Wales'.

Timmermans (1997) 'Correlates of Happiness in 42 Nations: Analysis of the World Values Study 1900–1991'. URL: worlddatabaseofhappiness.eur.nl/correlational-findings/9007/

UKHSA (2022) 'Heat mortality monitoring report: 2021'. URL: gov.uk/government/publications/heat-mortality-monitoring-reports/heat-mortality-monitoring-report-2021

UNEP (2009) *From Conflict to Peacebuilding: The role of natural resources and the environment.* URL: iisd.org/publications/conflict-peacebuilding-role-natural-resources-and-environment

UNHCR (2012) 'Protecting people crossing borders in the context of climate change: Normative gaps and possible approaches'. URL: unhcr.org/4f33f1729.pdf

Villani, D., Sorgente, A. et al. (2019) 'The role of spirituality and religiosity in subjective well-being of individuals with different religious status'. *Frontiers in Psychology* 9 July 2019. URL: frontiersin.org/articles/10.3389/fpsyg.2019.01525/full

Welsh Government (2022) 'A guide to the Well-being of Future Generations Act'. URL: gov.wales/sites/default/files/publications/2022-04/easy-read-a-guide-to-the-wellbeing-of-future-generations-act-april-2022.pdf

World Commission on Environment and Development (1987) Our Common Future. URL: sustainabledevelopment.un.org/content/documents/5987our-common-future.pdf

Acknowledgements

This book has been a long time coming. Although I had the idea several years ago, I've been mulling over it for quite a while. In the course of that mulling, lots of people have helped shape my ideas into the book you're reading now. Those people broadly form into three groups who I'd like to acknowledge.

First, all my friends, work colleagues and sometimes strangers over the years who have taken the time to discuss the topics in this book. They've allowed me to explore the ideas, to write about them and to speak on the subject. I'm grateful for those who have been supportive. I'm also grateful to those who have challenged the ideas because this has allowed me to mould the concept into a real thing. So thank you to you all.

Second, I'd like to thank all the researchers and scientists who have carried out the basic research to prove that there is a concept of measuring happiness. This really lends authority to the idea and hopefully will lead to the concept being adopted worldwide and hence to a better world.

Finally, and by no means least, I'd like to thank the editing and publishing team at The Right Book Company. I am not a natural writer and their support has been invaluable. I really like the dedication they have taken to 'get' the idea, even though it slightly defies categorisation. Their editing and proofreading have been gratefully received. That said, if there are any difficult to understand sentences or errors then they are mine and not theirs.

About the author

Richard Lupo is a chartered environmentalist and managing director of SHIFT, a company that drives sustainability through environmental reporting and related consultancy. A full member of the Institute of Environmental Management and Assessment (IEMA), Richard has carried out scores of sustainability assessments for a variety of clients, including social housing landlords, councils, developers, care homes and wealthy individuals. He is proud that his work is leading to significant environmental and value for money improvements.

Richard has also trained and qualified more than 300 Code for Sustainable Homes assessors and has trained building professionals on Housing Quality Indicators and sustainable refurbishment. He is an ESOS lead assessor and his key skills are calculating carbon emissions and the technical side of research. His particular expertise is developing and instigating streamlined processes to ensure environmental effectiveness.

Richard has a degree in metallurgy gained from the University of Nottingham and an MSc in environmental engineering from Imperial College London. While at ICL he developed a waste silt recycling process and studied the impact of new regulations on hazardous waste disposal.

Richard has had a lifelong interest in sustainability issues, including the impact on wellbeing. He is qualified for wellbeing assessments using the WELL AP scheme and as part of the Code for

Sustainable Homes and Home Quality Mark schemes. In his spare time, Richard researches the connections between environmental protection and meeting human needs and wellbeing. He lives in Stroud.